DCPL0000184962

D0241927

Behind the Horseshoe Bar

At Dublin's Shelbourne Hotel

Behind the Horseshoe Bar

At Dublin's Shelbourne Hotel

Sean Boyd

BLACKWATER PRESS

Editor: Claire Rourke

ISBN 978-0-9563541-0-5

© Blackwater Press, 2009

BWP Ltd., 1 North Frederick Street, Dublin 1.

Printed in the Republic of Ireland.

The author would like to the following for giving their kind permission to reproduce photographs: Alan Devlin, Barry O'Callaghan and Noel Pearson, courtesy of *The Irish Times*. Oliver Reed, © Corbis Sygma. Richard Harris, Time & Life Pictures/Getty Images. John Hurt, Getty Images. Gerry Danaher, P.J. Mara and Gerry Ryan, courtesy of Photocall Ireland. Michael O'Sullivan, James Gibbons and Dr John Wallace, courtesy of Mary P. O'Connor.

While every effort has been made to contact copyright holders, we may have failed to contact some. Blackwater Press will be happy to come to some arrangement with these should they wish to contact us.

The poem 'Wintered' on page 94 is reproduced by kind permission of the poet, John McNamee.

Contents

Acknowledgements   *vii*

The Most Distinguished Address in Ireland:
A Short History of the Shelbourne Hotel *by* Michael O'Sullivan   1

Sean Boyd's Belfast and Dublin Days   10

'The Relics of Auld Dacency': The Early Days of the Horseshoe Bar   20

Reflections from the Looking Glass: A Cast of Thousands   28

Cocktails   117

Index   135

Acknowledgements

I am grateful for the time, support and practical assistance that I was given, in great amounts, by Helen Hardy, John Moran, Etain Boyd, Daragh Boyd, John McNamee, Ian McGlinchey, Oliver Caffrey and the Guinness Storehouse.

I am grateful to Michael O'Sullivan for contributing the historical introduction, to James Gibbons of the *Daily Mail* and to Mary P. O'Connor for providing photographs.

I would like to thank the owners of the Shelbourne Hotel and the management team from the Marriott Group. Thanks also to the council of the UK Bartenders Guild for permission to use 'The History of the Cocktail', as published in the 1965 edition of the UKBG *Guide to Drinks*.

Sean Boyd
September 2009

To my family and all those who came through
the door of the Horseshoe Bar.

Chapter One

The Most Distinguished Address in Ireland:

A Short History of the Shelbourne Hotel
by Michael O'Sullivan

An Irish Legend

SINCE IT FIRST opened its doors to the public in 1824, the Shelbourne Hotel has held a unique position in the commercial and social life of Dublin. It would not be too large a claim to say that few Irish hotels have exercised an influence as all embracing as that held by the Shelbourne. This was clearly evident in the mid-1990s when a rumour circulated in the city that the then owners intended to change the hotel's name. Letters of protest were written to the national newspapers. Irate callers inundated the radio talk shows with furious comments. The Shelbourne's manager had to calm the storm by giving a guarantee that no name change was about to take place. Similarly, there were plans made during the days of the hotel's ownership by the Forte Group to completely alter the interior of the Horseshoe Bar, which evoked a wave of protest from many quarters. Lord Forte was even buttonholed in the House of Lords and asked what his intentions were. Why does this hotel, for many years known as 'the grand old lady of St Stephen's Green', evoke such passionate feelings among such a wide range of people, irrespective of age, class or background?

At a time when nearly all of Dublin's old hotels have passed into history, the Shelbourne has come to be seen as the flagship of tradition in Dublin. Its landmark position has aided its claim to fame, rather like other old hotels in European capitals. Continuity plays a large role in the affirmation process. Great cities are defined by the longevity of their institutions. Glamour, too, plays a role. The Shelbourne has always evoked images of glamour whether it was James Cagney dancing on the piano in the Drawing Room, Peter O'Toole bathing in Shelbourne champagne or Bono singing in the Horseshoe Bar. For nearly 200 years, the Shelbourne has been a silent witness to the events happening within its walls.

There is also the emotive issue of the history of the hotel running in tandem with the history of the emerging Irish state. At every major moment of Ireland's recent history, the hotel has played host to momentous events happening in the capital. It was occupied by British forces during the 1916 Rising and then by Free State forces during the Civil War. When a truce was declared in 1922, it was to the Shelbourne that the leaders of the new Ireland, under Michael Collins, came to write the first constitution of a free and independent Ireland. In the 1950s, the leadership of the country, under Taoiseach Seán Lemass, began to entertain in the hotel, giving it the benediction of the new order. During the Troubles in Northern Ireland, the Shelbourne became a victim when it suffered serious bomb damage. Even very recently, secret talks on the future of the peace process in the North were held quietly within the Shelbourne. To many, it seemed that there could never be a moment in the development of Ireland in which the Shelbourne could not play a significant role. Affection for our ancient traditions runs deep in the consciousness of the Irish psyche. At a time of great change in the physical make-up of the capital in the past few decades, the Shelbourne has come to represent continuity.

Early Days

The Shelbourne was founded in 1824 by Tipperary man Martin Burke. He was a self-made, Catholic businessman of remarkable entrepreneurial acumen. It is necessary to mention his religion only because the repressive laws which hindered the progress of Catholics in business in Ireland had been repealed only five years before the Shelbourne was opened. Burke was in the first wave of the new order of Irish-Catholic businessmen. He had remarkable foresight and saw that the extension of the railway to the suburbs of Dublin would make the way clear for the building of houses in these areas. From money accumulated in this way, he bought a group of Georgian buildings at the Kildare Street end of St Stephen's Green. His reason for opening the hotel was simply to provide accommodation for grand county families, who did not own a Dublin townhouse, for use during the social season. That world revolved around life in Dublin Castle which was then the centre of British administration in Ireland.

So, in its early days, the Shelbourne was not a conventional hotel in the sense that we know it today but rather it contained suites of rooms and a communal Drawing Room and Dining Room for wealthy patrons who needed a Dublin base to further their social and political ends.

Opening

Initially, the hotel was known simply as 'Burke's' but with a view to gaining the patronage of the wealthy gentry and aristocracy, Martin Burke decided to call the hotel after the second Earl of Shelburne. Many people ask why the 'o' was added to the name of the hotel. It appears to have only one possible explanation: when the sign for the hotel was being written across the exterior of the three Georgian houses that then constituted the hotel, the man doing the job felt there was too much space and added the extra 'o', thus creating the name that has gone down in history. Within weeks of opening, the hotel was an immediate success and within its first twenty-five years, it was established as one of the best hotels in Ireland. This called for expansion and Burke purchased more houses on Kildare Street and Stephen's Green. By the time of his death in 1863, the Shelbourne was so famous that it had been immortalised in the writings of Thackeray and was known throughout Europe for its stylish service.

The New Shelbourne

By February 1866, nothing remained of the original Shelbourne buildings. Martin Burke's widow sold the hotel to a consortium called Jury, Cotton and Goodman and the hotel as we now know it was born. The leasehold interest was sold for £13,000. The first requirement was for a new building and the Irish Victorian architect, John McCurdy and the builder Samuel Bolton were engaged to build a hotel that would equal in stature the great hotels of London and Paris

It seems hard to believe today that the range of buildings containing the Shelbourne was completed in ten months. The hotel extended 126 feet along Stephen's Green and 175 feet down Kildare Street and cost £73,000. Three hundred men worked alternate shifts around the clock to finish the great edifice. Contemporary reports describe how the citizens of Dublin looked on in amazement as the Shelbourne began to rise against the skyline.

Architectural Features

The exterior architecture was described by the architect as Renaissance in style. The walls are of red brick which complimented the neighbouring Georgian houses. The main exterior features are of Portland stone and the building is cross-banded in cream painted stucco. The entrance porch with its glass canopy was added later. If you wish to imagine McCurdy's pure concept just think of the façade without the canopy. The double bay windows rise to the height of the reception rooms on the first floor and were intended for the viewing of parades. A scroll-patterned balustrade in cast iron protects this area of the building.

The most prominent exterior decorative feature is the four bronze statues on their granite plinths. The two nearest the main door represent Egyptian princesses. The two flanking the corners are Nubian slave girls. They are very much in the style fashionable in Paris of the time were cast in the French capital from models made by Frenchman M.M. Barbezet and were cast in Paris. They are jokingly known to generations of Dubliners as 'the last four virgins in Dublin'.

Inside, the hotel contained only fifteen bedrooms. Most were 23 feet by 17 feet and had adjoining sitting rooms 29 feet by 23 feet. A Smoking Room, Billiards Room, Coffee Room and several Dining Rooms and Turkish bath added to the style of the hotel.

Everything in the interior spoke of high Victorian style. Chimney-pieces were of carved Carrara marble and Valentia slate. Rich wall hangings and Turkish carpets were complimented by furniture bought in London. The hotel was lit by gas light which had first come to Dublin in 1825. By 1881, the hotel was illuminated by electricity. It was now not only the grandest hotel in Ireland but one of the grandest in Europe. The Shelbourne also had the privilege of issuing its own stamps which consisted of a franking mark bearing the name of the hotel.

Sadly, John McCurdy, though a giant of his time, is largely forgotten today. Born in Dublin in 1823, he was architect to Trinity College Dublin and practised from offices in nearby Leinster Street where Samuel Beckett's father had his practice as a quantity surveyor. McCurdy was president of the Royal Irish Institute of Architects and died at the age of sixty-one. The Shelbourne Hotel building is his most enduring legacy.

The First Lady of the Shelbourne

For nearly a hundred years of its existence, the dominant name in the Shelbourne's history has been that of Jury, the family that founded the hotel group that still bears its name. Jury's originally stood on College Green. One name stands out in this famous clan of hotel owners and that is the irrepressible Margaret Cotton Jury. She was one of the most unusual women of her generation. In Victorian times, it was unheard of for a woman to run a business empire. Women could not vote or even hold a bank account in their own name. But Mrs Jury overcame all of this to rule the Shelbourne with an iron fist for thirty years. Her word and hers alone was law in the Shelbourne. She was fiercely loyal to her staff and defended them against all comers. This set a precedent that lasted for a century. A job at the Shelbourne, rather like a job at Guinness, was considered a job for life. In the course of her long life, Mrs Jury fought off several legal battles to ensure the Shelbourne was preserved, including battles with members of her own family. Finally, on 23 July 1896, she relinquished the reins of the hotel in favour of her son and her nephew. In her will, she left large bequests to Shelbourne staff and a hotel legacy and legend that has lasted into the present day.

A New Era at the Shelbourne

The departure of Mrs Jury heralded a new era at the Shelbourne. George Olden became the hotel's first manager, in the sense that we know the term today. It is to the talents of this man that the Shelbourne owes it survival. His reign at the hotel saw it through the end of the Victorian era to the emergence of the new, independent Irish state.

Olden's innovations brought the hotel into a new age. He installed the first lift in the hotel lobby, which necessitated changing the central staircase of McCurdy's original design. The imposing central flight was moved to the left to accommodate the new lift. The citizens of Dublin flocked to the hotel to see the new contraption. In 1907, a floor was added to the Kildare Street wing and the glass awning was added to the front entrance. When Olden took over in 1896, the hotel's receipts were £29,171, but, by 1907, they had risen to £46,374. Clearly, the Shelbourne had found its champion. Olden stayed on to see the hotel through the Great War, the 1916 Rising, the War of Independence and the Civil War. He steered the hotel through the early years of Irish independence and when the first draft of the Constitution of the Irish Free State was drawn up in Room 112, George Olden was presented with the first copy. He died in 1930 and the hotel's management passed to the grandson of Margaret Jury, Colonel E.C. Jury.

A Very Good War

Having survived the vicissitudes of major national and international conflicts, the Shelbourne faced its next great test, the Second World War. Irish neutrality meant expanded business for the Shelbourne. Officers on leave and their families, together with visitors escaping the rigors of wartime Britain, saw guest numbers rise radically. At the beginning of the war in 1939, guest numbers stood at about 20,000, by the end of the war, they were at 61,000. During these years, a regular visitor was the distinguished writer Elizabeth Bowen and it was at this time that she wrote her famous history of the hotel. Miss Bowen was the last in the line of Bowens of Bowen's Court, County Cork, and had made her mark as one of the most brilliant prose writers of her generation. She spent some time living in the hotel whilst researching the vast quantity of records which had recorded the daily activity of the hotel from the first day it opened. Elizabeth Bowen was friendly with Captain Peter Jury who ran the hotel on behalf of his family. There was a great deal of trust between the two and, therefore, Bowen was given access to all the financial records. Her book is very much a social history of Ireland as well as a history of a famous hotel and, on publication, became a bestseller. A second history was commissioned to mark the 175th anniversary in 1999.

Also at this time, the famous tenor, John McCormack, moved into the Shelbourne with his wife. They stayed for eighteen months adding to the glamour of wartime Shelbourne life. Adding to that glamour, too, was the famous English novelist Grahame Greene who conducted a secret affair at the Shelbourne with the fabulously wealthy and beautiful Catherine Walston, who was married to one of the richest men in England. As if all this was not enough, the Shelbourne played host to vast numbers of spies who made the hotel their wartime home.

Still in Family Hands

After the Second World War, the Shelbourne was run by Captain Peter Jury and it remained under his control until it passed from the Jury family to the Forte Group in the 1960s. Under his management, the Shelbourne expanded at an exponential rate and essentially the hotel, as it was until its recent closure for refurbishment, was his creation. He bought number 33 St Stephen's Green and added and developed the cocktail bar know as the Shelbourne Rooms. It was regarded as the most elegant cocktail bar in Dublin and, until the Horseshoe Bar opened in 1957, was the hotel's main centre of activity. During Peter Jury's years, the hotel began to reflect the emergence of the new social order in Ireland. Gone were the old aristocratic voices barking orders at waiters and porters. The members of the emerging Irish business class were the new patrons.

To satisfy the need for large functions, a Ballroom was added in 1955, and Noël Coward attended the opening night. Earl Gill and his band became the resident musicians and the Great Room resounded to the sound of the waltz, tango and foxtrot, and jazz. The new ballroom was designed by the distinguished architect Michael Scott who also designed a new Grill Room, later known as the Sidedoor Restaurant. During this time, the Shelbourne also played host to another long-term resident, the soprano Margaret Burke Sheridan, one of the most famous opera divas of the day.

A Twenty-Three Stone Queen

In 1953, the Shelbourne played host to Queen Salote of Tonga. She had just attended the coronation of Queen Elizabeth II in London and wanted to spend two nights in Dublin. There was one major problem for the hotel. Queen Salote weighed twenty-three stones and no bed in the hotel could accommodate her.

With only three days' notice, a special bed was made and put in place in time for her arrival. Queen Salote arrived with a vast staff including her two personal chefs. Later, John F. Kennedy and his wife Jacqueline slept in that famous bed as did Rock Hudson, Peter O'Toole and Harold Wilson. Another regular guest at that time was Princess Grace of Monaco after whom the hotel's principal suite was named.

End of the Old Era and the Beginning of the New

In 1960, the link with the Jury family and Irish ownership was essentially broken and the Shelbourne came under the control of the Trust House Forte Group. Peter Jury remained on in a titular role for several years but the major decisions affecting the hotel were now made in London. As always because of the extraordinary nature of the relationship between its patrons and the Shelbourne, life went on as normal despite the ownership change. It's as if the old hotel had a life of its own. The swinging sixties brought prosperity to the Shelbourne and to Ireland. The era of new business was ushered in by a new Taoiseach Seán Lemass whose focus was on bringing Ireland forward as a modern, progressive nation. Central to this prosperity was the Shelbourne's restaurant, the Saddle Room, famous for its roast beef. On any day of the week, you could see the captains of industry and politicians taking up their favourite tables. Charles Haughey was a regular as was Tony O'Reilly and a host of up-and-coming business and political personalities. It was the most popular dining spot in Dublin.

Changing tastes in the 1970s and 1980s were accommodated at the Shelbourne. The hotel has never stood in the way of progress and has embraced change not as a challenge but as a welcome adventure. The hard political realities have never been far from the Shelbourne's door. In 1974, the hotel manager was threatened by bomb attacks if he did not hand over £60,000 to an unknown terrorist group. In 1976, a terrorist bomb exploded in the hotel causing severe damage and had it not been for the vigilance of the staff, several lives would have been lost. The 1980s were a difficult time for the hotel when recession gripped the Irish economy. In 1983, an industrial dispute lasting three months hit the hotel severely. So serious were its effects that after the return to work, the Grill Room, the Saddle Room and the Paddock Bar were all closed. However, there was good news, too, in the 1980s. *Newsweek International* voted the Horseshoe Bar one of the top 100 bars in the world. In 1989, the Ballroom was remodelled to its present design. Money was spent on the upgrading of bedrooms and public areas and, in 1991, the Saddle Room became the Shelbourne Bar.

Also in 1991, Trust House Forte became Forte plc and, in 1994, it bought the Meridien Group, which became the management company of the Shelbourne. Later, the Granada Group acquired Forte and the Shelbourne passed into its control, with Meridien still at the helm. In 2004, the hotel was bought by a consortium of Irish businessmen and the hotel came, once again, under Irish ownership under the management of the Marriott Group, and so began a new phase in the history of a hotel always willing to take on the banner of change.

Chapter Two

Sean Boyd's
Belfast and Dublin Days

"The bricks they may bleed and the rain it may weep
And the damp Lagan fog lulls the city to sleep.
It's to Hell with the future, we'll live in the past
May the Lord in his mercy be kind to Belfast."

Maurice James Craig

I WAS BORN IN Belfast on 18 June 1943. At that time, the city was being torn apart more by international than local strife. The year before my birth, the US army had joined the other military occupying force and the city – and the province – settled in for a rather bad war. Over a thousand people were killed in the Belfast blitz and one quarter of the city's population was left homeless. Northern Ireland was of strategic importance as it had the key shipyards manufacturing for the war effort. The detailed weather reports collected by Spitfires flying high over the province were of crucial significance. When I was three years old, General George Patton came to Belfast. With his pair of pearl-handled pistols and his specially designed helmet, he was a magical figure for a young boy. He stood like some western movie icon on the steps of City Hall and unveiled a monument to the US forces. Many years later, I would welcome his great-niece to the Shelbourne Hotel in Dublin. But that forms an altogether different part of this story.

My family lived in Kimberley Street off the Ormeau Road. My parents, John and Pauline Boyd, had four children – three boys, Tommy, Conor and myself, and one girl, my sister, Cecilia. Wartime rationing was not of particular concern to a small boy – sweets and fresh fruit were not very freely available until some years later and we did not miss what we didn't really know. I later became aware of my mother's concerns about ration coupons and of running a household at a time of frugality but there were many who were worse off than we were. My mother was known as a great provider, not just for her own family but also for many others. She was a woman of generous nature and her brother, my uncle John, who owned the Harbour Lights Bar in at 6 Echlin Street, just off James Street in Dublin, supplied her with all the goods that were rationed in Belfast during the war and immediately after. He regularly took the train from Dublin to Belfast, laden down with goods but he made sure to bring a half-bottle of whiskey for the conductor to smooth the passage of so many goodies going north. My mother then passed on as much of the surplus as she could to our needy neighbours and, in the process, taught us an important lesson in life.

My mother was born in Silvermines, Nenagh, County Tipperary. My father was from Carrick-on-Shannon in County Roscommon. It was a connection to that town that secured my father's first job in Belfast in the Royal Avenue Hotel. It belonged to the Burke family from Carrick-on-Shannon. When the hotel closed in the late 1940s, my father set up his own business, a shop on the Dublin Road which carried the Boyd family name. Our family home also moved to Dublin Road, the road that would later carry me out of Belfast for good.

I cannot lay claim to have had idyllic or halcyon schooldays. Oxford Street CBS was hardly the Eton of the North, but my own indifference to scholarship, coupled with a dreamy disposition, is where the fault mostly rested. My great joy in those days was the simple pleasure in serving mass. I was a born altar boy. My church was St Malachy's in the Markets area, though I had been christened in the Holy Rosary Church, Ormeau Road. At St Malachy's, Archdeacon McAuley became my mentor. Every morning, at 7 a.m., I served his mass and, every Saturday, he gave me half-crown (or a half dollar as we called it). Remembering this, reminds me of a story told in the Shelbourne many years later. Before independence, the crown solicitor was accosted outside the hotel by a lady of the night who asked the obvious question, 'Hey, mister, are ya doing business?' His was response was,

'Madam, I am the crown solicitor.' Her retort, 'Never mind, luv, sure I'm the half-crown solicitor!' I'm sure Archdeacon McAuley would have been horrified!

Archdeacon McAuley used to celebrate very quiet wedding masses at a side altar of St Malachy's in what even to my young mind seemed curious circumstances. There would be the bride and groom, two witnesses, the priest and myself. They were hasty affairs. When I asked my parents about them, my youthful inquisitiveness was met with stony silence. Later, the archdeacon explained that if one of the parties was a non-Catholic, it was the rule to marry them at the side altar, away from the prying eyes in the main body of the church. It was also the custom to do this if the bride was pregnant. Many of the couples who entered mixed marriages often did so in secret and returned separately to the homes of their parents, only living together as husband and wife later.

As older children, we were told stories of the horrors of the war on individual Belfast families. Many from that time can recall the harrowing sight of an open coffin containing the body of a young mother with a dead baby in each arm. Or the heart-touching sight of the open coffin of a beautiful young girl in her first communion dress; all victims of a terrible war and a foretaste of even more terrible times to come.

'The blighting city' is how the novelist Bernard McLaverty describes Belfast at this time. He also uses the term 'desolate' to describe my hometown in the post-war period. There was, of course, the strong and crippling sense of a Catholic underclass deprived of access to the better jobs and housing and unable to break through the bigoted carapace of religious division. Just months before I was born, there was quite a shock to Unionist sensibilities when Jack Beattie of the Northern Ireland Labour Party took a safe Unionist seat in the Belfast West by-election. However, it would be a very long time before the old order would change in any significant way or yield to Francis Davis' sentiment when he wrote:

> *We've been riven,*
> *We've been riven,*
> *The crafty spoiler's prey,*
> *But your Ulstermen,*
> *And Orangemen,*
> *Are Irishmen today.*

My early Belfast days were free of the sectarianism of later years. My parents never spoke of Protestants as being any different to the rest of us. In the respective parts of the republic from which they came, they got on well with their Protestant neighbours and their attitude in the North was guided by what they had experienced in the South. Our family holidays were spent with my father's people at Carrick-on-Shannon. It was not unusual for us to move there for the whole summer where, as city kids, we could enjoy the unbridled freedom of the Irish countryside.

I remember my father telling me that Carrick-on-Shannon was the ancient territory of both the O'Rourke clan of Breffni and their great rivals the Reynolds clan. Stories of their territorial battles were part of my childhood as if they had happened only yesterday. I remember looking at the remains of Carrick Castle and imagining the terrible deeds that must have happened in its shadow. I was also enchanted by the boats on the Shannon as they sailed passed majestically, vast galleons in the eyes of a little boy.

I was in the habit of wandering off alone in the lanes around Carrick much to the dismay of my grandfather, Tom Boyd. Sometimes we walked together and, during these walks, he would explain to me the various origins and lore surrounding the holy wells and places of interest. These holy wells were places of pilgrimage where the poor and those of happy and simple faith found solace in the expression of their beliefs. We also used to walk around the old Rockingham Estate on Lough Key, a reminder of the days of the old Irish Raj. The estate belonged to the Stafford-King-Harman family, descendants of the Earls of Kingston. I can remember the towering, gothic gate lodge which was so grand and impressive as it extended over the entrance gates. There was also a romantic ruin of an old Mac Dermot castle on an island opposite the house. My grandfather told me that the local IRA raided the house for guns during the War of Independence. It was burned in an accidental fire in 1957 and later was demolished by the state, which turned Rockingham into a forest park.

It was on these walks with my grandfather, returning from Rockingham, that I came to know a kind and decent man called Paddy Lenihan. He entertained us in his cottage or we would watch him saving turf for his winter fire. He was the grandfather of our current president, Mary McAleese.

Back in Belfast, I left Oxford Street CBS and moved to Harding Street CBS, a small technical school of about 200 students. My indifference to scholarship remained as steadfast there as it had always been. It was here that I met a charming but firm schoolmaster, Jim Aitken, who would cross my path again in later life when he became the founder of the legendary music promotion empire, Aitken Promotions.

In 1959, I came to Dublin and stayed with my uncle at his bar in Echlin Street. I enjoyed helping out being the counter and began to think that I would very much like to train as a professional barman. While I was in Dublin, I receive an invitation to the 200th anniversary party for Arthur Guinness & Co. It was a glamorous evening in July 1959 with representatives of the vintners trade and members of the Guinness family, many of whom would also cross my path in later life. Draught Guinness had just been launched in Ireland and I remember the early advertising campaigns, one of which had the motto 'the first 200 years are the hardest!'. I also recall seeing the issue of two commemorative postage stamps bearing the head of Arthur Guinness, a sure sign that the pint of plain was finally recognised as 'yer only man'.

In 1961, I returned to Belfast, more particularly to the Newtownards Road area, with the intention of completing the five-year apprenticeship in my chosen profession. This began with the Irish Bonding Company, which had been founded in 1951 and was later bought by Guinness. From there, I moved to White's Tavern Wine Cellar in High Street to complete my period of apprenticeship. White's had the feeling of an ancient inn and it lays claim to a foundation date of 1630. From this venerable seat of Belfast imbibing, I moved to work for Tommy Hunt in the Star and Garter on Rosemary Street where I remained for the remainder of the 1960s, until the events that would change the face of Northern Ireland intervened to chart a completely new and unexpected course in my own life.

Those years at the Star and Garter were happy and made happier by the arrival of a new director and by my own promotion to manager of the complex of bars which consisted of the main bar, the Rosemary Rooms and the Red Barn. The new director was Paddy Lenihan, namesake and son of the man I used to visit with my grandfather after those walks on the Rockingham Estate. His daughter, and Ireland's future president, Mary McAleese, worked part-time at the bar when she was a law student at Queen's University.

While at the Star and Garter, I entered and won my first cocktail competition and won first prize at the Bisquit de Bouche competition. The year was 1967. The competition was held in the Royal Hibernian Hotel in Dublin, a place where I later worked and it was the first time a Northern Irish barman had won a major all-Ireland award for cocktails. My winning cocktail was called a Rosemantic and the recipe for it may be found with the other cocktails at the end of this book.

Just two years later, my joyous victory in Dublin was put very much in the shade by my first close encounter with sectarian hatred. In August 1969, the face of Northern Ireland changed forever. The facts are well known. From 13–17 August, Northern Ireland was shaken by intensive sectarian violence. Belfast was most seriously hit in response to the Battle of the Bogside in Derry which saw the beleaguered Catholic nationalist population defend themselves against the Royal Ulster Constabulary. Eight people were killed in Belfast, hundreds were injured and thousands driven from their homes. There are now numerous scholarly accounts describing what happened, below is one account of the immediate aftermath of those days:

> *Eight people had been killed and 750 injured, of whom 133 (72 Catholics and 61 Protestants) were treated for gunshot wounds. Since many people would have been unwilling to report bullet wounds for fear of police attention, the true total may be higher again. In addition a total of 1,505 Catholic families and 315 Protestant ones were expelled from their homes, either through burning or intimidation. A further 275 commercial premises were badly damaged or destroyed, of which 83% were Catholic.*
>
> *The riots represented the most sustained violence that Northern Ireland had seen since the early 1920s. Protestants and unionists believed the violence showed the true face of the Civil Rights movement – as a front for the IRA and armed insurrection. Catholics, on the other hand, saw the riots, particularly in Belfast, as an assault on their community, in which the forces of the state had appeared as anything but neutral.*

These events are recognised as the beginning of the 'Troubles'. However, it was my own personal encounter with the sectarian hatred that drove me from my home town.

The Star and Garter was conveniently located for shipyard workers on their way home from the famous Harland and Wolff shipyards. Most of my shipyard patrons called in to the bar between 4.40 p.m. and 7 p.m., Monday to Friday. They were a very good-humoured crowd of men and I never had any problems with them. In August 1969, that all changed. It was about a week after the Troubles had started and, as was the case every Thursday evening, we had the shipyard men in the house – but, this particular evening, something seemed different. There was a heavy atmosphere in the place. I had my back to the bar counter when I was suddenly pushed to the floor by one of my staff. A very large glass ashtray came hurtling over the bar and smashed into a mirror behind where I had been standing. I picked myself up and looked at the motionless faces staring back at me amid the eerie silence. I ordered my staff out from behind the bar counter and told the customers that the bar was closed. I stood at the end of the bar – which was one of those old Victorian types with a long mahogany counter – and held on to it so that no one could see me shaking. If I had shown any sign of weakness, I felt all might have been lost and instead of an incident, there might be a full-scale mêlée. The bar cleared very quickly. I closed up and organised transport to get my staff home.

At this time, I was living in Turf Lodge at the top of the Falls Road. I decided that, from the next day, I would close the bar at 4 p.m. every day. I was unable to get in touch with my bosses, to let them know what was happening as no one was answering the telephone. It was about six months later that we closed the Star and Garter for good. We felt it was too dangerous for the staff. Suddenly, and for the first time in its history, it now mattered that the Star and Garter was a Catholic bar. It was just another sad sign of the troubles that were to come.

By the time the Star and Garter closed, I was qualified and experienced in the management of public houses. In 1971, I went to work in the Pig n'Chick'n in Temple Patrick in County Antrim. It was a fun place that never seemed to close. One of our doormen was Derek Davis, a tall, burly man who later became famous as a RTÉ broadcaster.

The Troubles carried on, not always at the pace Belfast had seen in 1969 but, in many ways, more dangerous for those of us trying to continue with our daily lives. I lived eleven miles from the Pig n'Chick'n but, to get home, it was best never to travel the same road twice in one week. It was considered too dangerous. Some nights, I would travel a circuitous route that varied between eleven and fifty miles, just to get home. I was about to get married to Josephine, who was living in Dublin at the time. I had met Josephine, who was from Ballinahinch, County Down, in Belfast in 1967 when she was working as a bridal consultant in The Spinning Mill. She moved to Dublin in 1969, when the Troubles were at their height and worked in Penny's on O'Connell Street and Roches Stores on Henry Street. We married in 1973 and have two children, Etain and Daragh.

Very late one night in the Pig n'Chick'n, I was in the Kitchen Bar when several RUC men came in, steaming drunk. I served them a couple of drinks. They were getting very boisterous so I told them I wasn't going to serve them anymore. One policeman put his hand in his pocket and banged his hand on the counter. When he opened it there were five bullets in the palm of his hand. He said, 'One of those had got your name on it.' I excused myself, left the bar and went up to the office where my boss, Sean Gallagher, was sitting. I told him what had happened and asked him to send on what money I was due. I left there and then and never returned to that pub. I went straight home, changed my clothes, got in the car and drove through the night to Dublin.

Dublin in 1974 was a very different place to what it is today. The onset of middle age quite often lends itself to view the past through rose-coloured spectacles. I don't subscribe to the notion of 'it was always better in the old days'. Quite often, it was miserable in the old days. Jobs were very scarce but now, in recession-struck Ireland, they are scarce again. Unemployment was a serious problem; now it is a serious problem again. People were leaving the country at a furious pace; and now they are doing so again. They cyclical theory of history has a curious and unforgiving way of proving itself correct.

When I had settled in Dublin, I met quite a few of my friends from Belfast who had moved south, amongst them Derek Davis who I bumped into on one of my first days in my new town. He told me that he had just been for an interview with RTÉ. Another was Sammy Smyth, the journalist and author, who was to become one of the top investigative reporters in Ireland. He was also to become the Boswell par excellence of pre- and post-Celtic Tiger Ireland. I knew Sammy well in Belfast. He was the manager of one of the Top Ballrooms in Queen Street. He was also the editor of *Spotlight* magazine, the first of its kind in Ireland to chronicle the world of popular music and showbands and the early days of pop culture. He also managed a few showbands.

A friend of mine, Jim Gallagher, tells a great story about Sammy. Jim ran a very popular ballroom called The Boathouse and had booked a band managed by Sammy and, on the grapevine, Jim heard that the same band was booked elsewhere the same evening. Jim could not find Sammy and Sammy was not answering the telephone, so Jim decided that he would call Sammy just at the time when he would be getting home at about 4 a.m. He phoned and, as predicted, the phone was answered. Down the line came these words, 'S-s-s-s-ammy S-s-s-myth's N-o- n –o – not home' and then the line went dead. This was long before phone-answering services or answering machines had been heard of. Sammy remains a good friend and a man bothered by telling a story against himself.

Dublin in the 1970s was just about catching up on the earlier decade of 'swinging sixties' London. The concept of the cocktail bar had already arrived in the capital but new to Dublin was the notion of the formica and fluorescent neon bar which were about to open in spades about the town. I decided my career should take me on to the more sedate world of the genteel hotel, and I applied for a job in the Royal Hibernian Hotel in Dawson Street.

The hotel was always referred to in Dublin as 'the old Hibernian'. By the time I started working there in 1978, it had achieved a venerable status. It was founded in 1751 and its principal competition came from the nearby Shelbourne Hotel (1824) which, together with the old Hibernian, had been bought by the Forte Group by the time I arrived. Architecturally, it consisted of an amalgamation of a group of Georgian houses on Dawson Street facing up Molesworth Street towards the impressive façade of the Duke of Leinster's town residence, which now houses the Irish parliament. The Hibernian had, in its early day, been a Bianconi coaching inn. Charles Bianconi revolutionised public transport in Ireland in the nineteenth century, when he founded a network of coaching routes that crossed Ireland from Belfast to Cork from a point that began at Hearn's Hotel in County Tipperary. The Hibernian had a basement grill which it named after Charles Bianconi.

The Hibernian was the last bastion of the old Anglo-Irish families. It nearest London equivalent would be the Connaught in Carlos Place, Mayfair. You could still hear the loud, confident tones of the remnants of the landed gentry in the hotel's elegant public rooms. The Rotiserie and the Layfayette rooms were particular favourites of the patrons for dining and the upstairs cocktail lounge and the basement Buttery Bar were populated by the capital's rich and famous, as well as a host of visiting film stars and diplomats. The favourite spot for afternoon tea was under the dome in the Lobby.

At this time, the new Irish rich were beginning to feel more confident about coming to places like the Hibernian and the Shelbourne and they came in droves – this 'new' money quite soon became the young nation's 'old' money. Having secured a good job in the Hibernian, I felt my future in Dublin was secure and I settled down to getting to know a cast of thousands of characters that would form part of my life for over quarter of a century.

I spent four years in the Hibernian before it closed in 1982. I then applied for the vacant position of the barman in the Grill Bar at the Shelbourne and had an interview with the food and beverage manager. Elizabeth O'Neill, who was in charge of the Grill Bar, was called to the office and was asked, 'Do you think he will do?'

She looked at the manager and asked, 'Do we really need another barman?' My heart sank, I thought the job was gone. She then said, 'We can give him a trial', and the rest, as they say, is history. I began a job which brought me into contact with thousands of the most colourful and influential characters in Ireland.

Chapter Three

'The Relics of Auld Dacency':

The Early Days of the Horseshoe Bar

T HE SHELBOURNE FIRST opened its doors in times that were very different to those in which we now live. It was not a place for the greater Irish public to enjoy, but was to be a home away from home for the aristocracy and landed gentry – more a private club than a public hotel. It did not, for example, have a public bar when it was founded. In the nineteenth century, hotels were different institutions to what they are today and were not intended as a place to which people would casually drop in. However, by the time I started working there, there were some relics of 'auld dacency' left.

I remember the loud Anglo-Irish tones of Molly, Lady Cusack-Smith, sometime Master of the Galway Blazers and the Bermingham Hunt at Tuam, County Galway. It was she who famously quipped to a groom when he had remarked that her horse was in a terrible sweat 'my good man, if you had been between my legs for the past five hours, you too would be in a bit of a sweat'! Molly Cusack-Smith was an O'Rourke of the ancient clan O'Rourke and she married an English baronet, Sir Dermot Cusack-Smith. As a young woman, she had been a dress designer in London and Paris in the 1930s and had travelled to Moscow in the 1940s where she took inspiration for some of her designs. She drank her gin with just a splash of water. When she returned to Ireland, she settled at Bermingham House where she hosted the last hunt ball to be held in a private house in Ireland. The hunting class continued to support the Horseshoe Bar. The Louth Hunt Ball attracted large numbers to the hotel each year.

At one time or another almost all of the Guinness brewing clan, the Beerage as they were known, were patrons of the Horseshoe Bar. Oonagh Guinness, who married Lord Oranmore and Browne was a regular customer. One day, the portrait painter, Sean O'Sullivan saw her at the bar and said, 'Madam, I would like to paint you.'

To which came the reply, 'Why is that Mr O'Sullivan?'

He looked her ladyship straight in the eye and replied, 'Because you have an arse like an orangutan!'

For many years, her son, Gareth Browne was a regular patron of the bar. He was usually driven by a taxi driver from Bray called 'Batman'. Gareth's brother, Tara, was once voted one of the most beautiful men in the world. He was a friend of the Beatles, the Rolling Stones and the demimonde of London in the 'swinging sixties'. He married a local girl from County Wicklow but died tragically when he crashed his sports car in London not long after his twenty-first birthday. Those whom the gods love die young. The Beatles wrote the song 'A Day in the Life' about him. Tara Browne is buried at Luggala, County Wicklow, under a classical temple dome overlooking the lake where he spent his youth. His memory lives on and he was often spoken of in the Horseshoe Bar as though he were still there.

Gareth's circle of friends was wide and varied, many of them had rather odd nicknames which must have sounded strange to onlookers in the bar – 'The 'Shit Mackey' comes to mind immediately. He was a sort of antiques dealer who once sold Kevin McClory, of James Bond fame, a film projector which he claimed belonged to James Joyce. It appears 'The Shit' bought it on the quays of Dublin, scratched the initials 'J.J.' on it on the way to the Horseshoe Bar, then flogged it to McClory as an object of great literary veneration.

Another of Mr Browne's close friends was Count Randal McDonnell. When there was a sale of antiques at Luggala, the count was called upon to co-write a forward and help the auctioneers with the catalogue.

A flavour of the times is evident in an anonymous poem I found left behind in the Horseshoe Bar: It reads in part:

> *My Grandpa kept a yacht with 30 sailors*
> *His suits bespoke from ersatz London tailors.*
> *At his knee we learnt of Uncle Arthur*
> *Brewer, guru, rich man, hero, martyr.*
>
> *They sent me to a school called Le Rosey*
> *Where life was far from cheerful and from gay.*
> *So from its gates at 16 I did run*
> *Determined on a life of Gaelic fun.*
>
> *In Dublin town I found my true vocation*
> *Recording ancient songs throughout the nation.*
> *Old women in black shawls they worshiped me*
> *As they keened their fiddle-diddle-diddle-diddle-dee.*
>
> *I summoned up a homespun record label*
> *And sat my chums around a Georgian table.*
> *From morn 'till night we drank for inspiration*
> *'Till Claddagh's name arrived by pure gestation.*
>
> *I needed then a wife for this ménage*
> *So I travelled to the homeland of the Raj.*
> *Once there and free from Gaelic social scurvy*
> *I wed a daughter of the House of Morvi.*
>
> *Our billet soon became dear Luggala*
> *And ignoring every native crass guffaw,*
> *I proved to them I'm Irish and well got*
> *Dressed-up in Aran, in my Camelot.*
>
> *To Lugg' they came in legions rich and thick*
> *The Beatles, Bono, Marianne and Mick.*
> *They read from Heaney, Homer and The Táin*
> *And worshiped at the feet of Lord Bodhrán.*

Others in the Browne circle included Gloria McGowan, widow of the distinguished Beckett interpreter, Jack McGowan. The journalist Mary Finnegan, formerly Mrs Desmond Burke-Kennedy, who was also a keen huntswoman. The author and broadcaster Michael O'Sullivan who wrote biographies of Brendan Behan, Seán Lemass and Mary Robinson. There were great parties in the Shelbourne to launch these books as O'Sullivan was one of the hotel's nearest neighbours and friendly with many of the hotel's succession of general managers. I remember the party for the launch of his biography of Mary Robinson was so crowded that Mick Jagger was unable to get in to the room and listened to the speeches standing on the stairs. O'Sullivan always had a great turn of phrase and quick wit and was much liked by the staff.

Viscount Gormanston and his brother Roderic O'Connor were also regulars with Gareth Browne. Roderic is an expert on planning law and it was his expertise that prevented an interpretative centre being built at the very gates of Luggala. Another regular with Gareth was Desmond FitzGerald, the 29th Knight of Glin. The knight was Christie's representative in Ireland and brought many of his more distinguished clients to the Horseshoe Bar, often in the company of his beautiful wife Olda. He had been married to Loulou de la Falaise, who was the muse of Yves St Laurent.

The other great distilling families were also patrons of the bar. Most notable amongst them was the Williamses of Tullamore, famous for Tullamore Dew. They were represented by the always elegant Jane Williams who had a famous antiques shop near the Shelbourne. She was always stylishly dressed and I remember her wearing the most fabulous amber jewellery. Her father, Captain Jack Williams, who won the Military Cross, developed the Tullamore-based distillery into a world-class business. A cousin, Desmond Williams, married a daughter of Dr Oliver St John Gogarty, whose consulting rooms now form part of the Shelbourne buildings. Jane Williams can remember having lunch with Noël Coward at the Shelbourne when she was a young girl. Noël Coward was very friendly with two other great Horseshoe patrons, Micheál MacLíammóir and Hilton Edwards, the founders of the Gate Theatre.

Horseshow Week at the Royal Dublin Society usually brought in the remnants of the gentry who used to stay at the nearby Kildare Street Club in the days when its membership was made up mostly of the landed class and before it amalgamated with the University Club and moved from its impressive clubhouse on Kildare Street to St Stephen's Green. The amalgamation prompted Professor R.B. McDowell to say 'land and learning, they'll never mix'. The club hosted an annual cocktail party during horseshow week and the Horseshoe Bar was usually thronged with people, men in dinner jackets and ladies in elegant evening gowns on their way to one of many hunt balls. None was more elegant than Gareth Browne's great friend, the society beauty and art dealer Grace Pym, who restored the ancient Irish seat of the O'Carrolls of Ely near Roscrea. Grace sometimes came in with her friend the diminutive Johnny Lenihan, an ascendancy groupie, from Kanturk who looked like Andy Warhol but sounded like Truman Capote. His father was a local solicitor in Kanturk which in terms of provincial Irish small-town attitude in those days was the equivalent rank to a duke. His tutor in all things aesthetic was Kevin Coates from whom he learned about the finer things in life – art, furniture, silver and architecture. Johnny often came to the bar on his return from one his famous camping expeditions to Greece – a country to which he has been devoted for over half a century. He went there seeking beauty. He was often accompanied on his travels by one or other of his girlfriends to whom he was equally devoted. To the suprise of many, he never married. One such girl was Mary Geraldine O'Donnell known as the 'Countess of Donegal'. She was, in fact, from County Kerry and lived in London where she worked for *The Observer*. It was said of her that she was invited to every great house in England twice, the second time to apologise!

Kevin Coates was perhaps one of the more interesting of this circle. He had a very finely developed sense of the aesthetic which he used in the collection of art and furniture. He returned to Dublin from London where he had worked in the antiques business for many years. He very generously shared his knowledge with his friends and one often heard him leading a passionate debate on the need to save some great Irish house or other. He eventually gave up drinking altogether and spent his time travelling in his beloved Italy. His great friend was Hubert Hamilton, scion of a County Laois landed family and a former Guards officer who gave up his smart regimental life in England to return to Ireland to manage the family estate.

Hovering over all this Anglo-Irishry were Desmond Guinness and his wife Mariga. She was born into a German noble family and was related to half the royal houses of Europe. He was the son of Brian Guinness and Diana Mitford. Mariga was the principal motivating force behind the Irish Georgian Society which was founded in 1957. Her appearance and accent made her stand out among the crowd of Georgian tipplers in the Horseshoe Bar and it always seemed to me that she was rushing off to get a bucket of paint to begin the restoration process in some crumbling Georgian pile. She lived on Mountjoy Square but in her battles to save Georgian Dublin would often be found rallying her troops in the Horseshoe.

David Grenfell, that most affable of Old Etonians, was one of the best loved of the regular patrons. He moved with ease among a wide circle of the Anglo-Irish, having bought a large estate in County Wexford. He was married to Lucy Fox, daughter of the actor Edward Fox. Lucy Grenfell is now Lady Gormanston having married, secondly, Nicholas Gormanston an Irish peer who defended the Horseshoe Bar against a proposed architectural change which would have altered the very nature of the place altogether and obliterated Sam Stephenson's brilliant 1957 design. John Heather, an art dealer, was married to the sister of Lord Gormanston's first wife and was a regular Horseshoe Bar patron. He later married Henry Ford's step-daughter. When he was engaged to her David Grenfell nicknamed him 'the Ford Escort'. David Grenfell had the wittiest turn of phrase of almost any of the 1980s generation of customers in the bar. His booming, clippe

d, upper-class voice could be heard at the front door as he told stories of his shooting party exploits in the great estates of Ireland and England. He was extremely amusing about Noël Coward who was a friend of his mother and whenever he was in the bar a large circle of admirers would gather around him as he quaffed numerous Jameson whiskies and regaled the assembled company before sauntering off to a leisurely lunch at the nearby La Mère Zou. This French bistro became, at one stage, the favoured lunching retreat for many of the grander patrons of the bar. Gareth Browne had a regular table there where he entertained with his usual generosity. After lunch, many of the restaurant's patrons would troop back to the Horseshoe to continue the day's drinking until it was time to return to La Mère Zou for dinner. All of this was long before the days of the Celtic Tiger.

Lord Dunraven, wheelchair-bound, as a result of polio, but with undiminished spirit was also a regular. As was Lord Kilbracken, an ace fighter pilot and much decorated in the Second World War. He returned his medals to the Queen after the events of Bloody Sunday.

Donal Robinson Ryan, a scion of an old, landed Irish family has been a regular patron of the Horseshoe Bar for many years. It has been his almost reflex habit to drop in after Sunday service in St Patrick's or Christ Church and engage with old friends like Dr John Wallace, a most affable scholar with Trinity and Oxbridge connections and a man with encyclopaedic knowledge of the history of academe.

Mixed up with all this 'auld dacency' was a group of painters and poets. It was as if the eighteenth-century system of patronage was still alive. The painter Derek Hill was one such artist. He was, in Mark Bence-Jones's phrase, 'ascendancy by association'. He came in with Mariga Guinness. He was a friend of Elizabeth Bowen. He drank Punt e Mes, the Italian vermouth, and we kept a bottle especially for him. It was Derek Hill who, when told he was a terrible name dropper, replied in all seriousness, 'Do you know who said that to me at luncheon only yesterday? The Queen Mother.' He once left a London luncheon party, hosted by James Stafford, at the coffee stage, saying as he rose from the table, 'If you'll forgive me, James, I'm expected for coffee by the Queen Mother, whom I stood up to have luncheon with you today!' Stafford sent him a card next day saying, 'How the lowly have been exhalted over the mighty.'

Derek Hill taught both Noël Coward and the Prince of Wales to paint. Other painters came in from time to time. Camille Souter used to ask for 'a pony of ale' - a pony was half a half-pint measure. Louis le Broquy was also a regular for many years, as was Michael Farrell and many other artists, none more colourful or controversial than Mick Mulcahy, but we shall meet him later in this story.

This class about whom I write were rich men in a poor country, or perhaps they just appeared to be rich, perhaps they were rich in attitude and confidence. Their way of behaving was different. They had the confidence of their class and their public-school education. They were the class described by Brendan Behan as 'Protestants on horseback'. They were the Irish Raj, the Raj in the Rain, the ones who stayed on even after their houses had been burned out and their lands divided. They were the people of Elizabeth Bowen. They were seen as English in Ireland and Irish in England. I once heard one of their folk say in the bar that he felt like he was 'suspended in a hot-air balloon over the Irish Sea'. They wore faded old tweeds and their shirt cuffs were frayed. It was a look once described by author Michael O'Sullivan as 'full tweed ahead'. He also coined the phrase 'the stranded gentry' to describe them. They drove battered old cars and cared little for the trappings of appearance. Signet-ringed hands waved glasses about with the confidence acquired from centuries of knowing where they came from. They were resented by some and admired by others. Love them or hate them, they added colour and style to Dublin at a time when there wasn't much of it about.

As the change to the new, moneyed class of the Celtic Tiger began to happen the old order drifted away from the Horseshoe Bar. One day, I heard one of them say, 'What's that dreadful smell?', and, answering his own question, said, 'Ah, its new money.'

Chapter Four

Reflections from the Looking Glass:

A Cast of Thousands

BEING A GOOD barman is rather like being a good priest. The greatest similarity between the two callings is the need to keep the secrets of the confessional. People never cease to amaze me when it comes to what they will discuss at a bar counter, as if the barman is not there. I imagine it to be rather like the days of the Big House when the most intimate family business was discussed at the dinner table in front of the servants, as though they did not exist.

In Ireland, friendship is more like an invitation to a conspiracy than it is in England, where everyone shouts at the top of their voices so that nobody *actually* hears what anybody else is saying. In Ireland, people sit around whispering in huddled groups. At the Horseshoe, somehow, it was different. The nature of the acoustics are such that there are no secrets in the Horseshoe Bar. Coupled with this is the fact that it is, physically, really a hall of mirrors. From any one spot behind the bar, you have a complete view of what's happening in the room. The mirrors have been there since 1957 and what tales are contained in their mercury!

I have thought long and hard, and for many years, about how best to release some of the images witnessed by those mirrors during my time as their curator. This memoir covers a period in Irish social history from just before the birth of the Celtic Tiger to a time which saw that beast roaring wildly around the environs of the Shelbourne Hotel. I have, of course, encountered thousands of characters who have sauntered in to take a seat at the bar in my years as head barman. Some were more memorable than others. Some left a mark after only a few visits. Others attended with such regularity that they formed part of my extended family. All contributed to making the Horseshoe Bar one of the most fascinating places in Ireland.

The bar, itself, is a windowless, square room built in 1867, orignially as the reading and writing room of the old hotel. It had a very brief life as a television room before being converted to its present use in 1957 by Sam Stephenson and Aidan Prior. Stephenson had just left Bolton Street School of Architecture and Aidan Prior was then manager of Brown Thomas' contract interior department. They created a space that had an environment similar to that of a gentleman's club. It was painted dark red and that colour has been recently restored to replace the blue-green that another generation will remember. The horseshoe shaped bar was installed and to add to the slightly decadent atmosphere, its pediment was crowned with a panel of engravings of *A Rake's Progress* by William Hogarth. Not a splink of natural light enters the space and, as the Shelbourne history puts it, 'time and season in the Horseshoe are still best marked by the diurnal rhythms of the regular barflies'.

It was famously said of it that the bar was 'a place where women with a past met men with no future'. It was a place where love stories began and ended; a place where deals were made and broken; a place where fortunes were found and lost; a place where stories began and ended; a place where friendships were forged and destroyed; a place of myriad intrigues and a place where a cast of thousands played out their various roles. Here are pen portraits of some of the *dramatis personae*. They are not arranged in any particular order, as if, dear reader, I was sitting with you at the Horseshoe, telling a few good stories.

Oliver Reed – The Full Monty

Oliver Reed stayed in the hotel for a few days accompanied by a friend, a man of small stature who carried a bodhrán wherever he went. The first night Reed was in the bar, he started acting the fool and was promptly told by the staff that he would not be served if he carried on in that fashion. He left the bar a short time later and went over to O'Donoghue's on Merrion Row.

The following night, Reed was back in the Horseshoe with his little friend. At first, he was quite pleasant but, after a few drinks, his friend started banging on the bodhrán. I called Reed over and had a word with him about his friend's antics – I'd had to do the same the night before too. Oliver took a step back from me, took off his jacket, turned it inside out and started dancing around the bar accompanied by his little friend who was banging away on the bodhrán. At this point, he started to strip. I intervened. I took him to one side, he was laughing very loudly at me. I whispered in his ear, 'I am going to phone Josephine in Cork to let her know of your behaviour.' I made it very clear to him that I was not joking! He glared at me in a manner that frightened me for a minute – you were never sure about what he was capable of doing. Then, he stepped aside, buttoned up his shirt, took up his jacket, grabbed his little friend and left. People looked on in astonishment, wondering what I had said to him.

The next day, he returned again and asked me what I had meant about Josephine, who was his wife. I told him that she had phoned and told me that if I had any trouble with him, I was to call her and she would sort it out. Of course, this wasn't true. I had read an article in a magazine several years earlier in which he had said that he did not like her to know of his drink-related indiscretions as it upset her. He looked at me, unsure about whether or not to believe me. In the end, he apologised for his behaviour. The headlines in the *Evening Herald* that evening read: 'Oliver Reed Attempts the Full Monty in the Shelbourne'.

Louis XIII

One midwinter's Monday night, after a very quiet evening, I was closing up the bar. Three men entered. I told them that I was sorry but the bar was closed. They told me that they had just returned from a race meeting and pleaded with me for one last drink. One of the three left to go to the toilet and the other two approached me, saying that they had made no money at the races but their companion had made quite a lot, which was unfortunate as it was impossible to get a drink out of him. They then said that, when he returned, I was to say that I had agreed to give them a brandy each on him. The brandy in question was, of course, Louis XIII. I asked if they knew the price and they assured me that they did and that the bill would be settled one way or another. I sold them the three brandies, which amounted to £375.

As I was pouring the brandy, the chap who had ordered said to his friend, 'This is your round', to which his friend muttered something under his breath. He then pulled a wad of money out of his pocket and put two £20 notes on the counter. I stopped pouring and looked at him and asked him what they were for. 'The brandies,' he answered. I shook my head and told him that £40 would only cover his entitlement to look at the bottle; it would take another £330 to taste the contents. At this point, his friend stepped in and said, 'You're a miserable shit. You made a few bob today. You haven't bought a drink all day, but I'm making sure that you pay for this one.' The man reached back in to his pocket in disgust and took out the wad and peeled away the rest of the money, without including a tip. They lifted the brandies and swallowed them off in one go. I watched them and thought to myself that that was no way to treat a brandy of that calibre. Having finished their drinks, they promptly left the bar. A few moments later, one of them returned. He left £50 on the counter, smiled and left.

Another Louis XIII

A man in his early twenties walked in to the bar on another quiet winter's night and asked to speak with me. I asked him what I could do to help. He told me that he had just flown in from New York and, when he was in a taxi from the airport he'd asked the driver to take him to one of Dublin's top hotels. The taxi driver had taken him to the Berkeley Court. He had gone into the bar and had asked the bartender if he had such a thing as a bottle of Louis XIII. The bartender had told him he didn't know where the brandy could be bought at that time of the night. He had then told the man to go to the Horseshoe Bar in the Shelbourne and ask for Sean. 'If anyone has it, he has it,' the barman had said. I told the young man that I had exactly what he was looking for. The man said he would only buy it on condition that it was in the original box with the red velvet lining. I assured him that it was, stopper and all! At this, he agreed to take it without even asking the price. I told him that I would have to charge the bar price which meant charging him by the measure. He agreed to this without hesitation. I phoned the duty manager to get me a bottle from the cellar.

I asked the man if he was paying by cash or credit card. He told me he would pay by cash and took out a bundle of £20 notes. I took him into the back room to complete the transaction, to give him a bit more privacy. While we were counting out the money, I asked him what the occasion was. He told me about one of his friends who had worked with him on a building site in New York, who had become ill and was diagnosed with a terminal illness. When his friend had received his diagnosis, he had decided to go home to Kerry to die. This young man had promised his dying friend that he would one day stand at his graveside in Kerry and drink a brandy to him; this was what he was here to do – only the best brandy would do for his friend. When the bottle arrived up from the cellar, I put it into his rucksack. I suggested putting something to the side of it to stop it moving about in the bag, to which he replied, 'Put in a bottle of Jameson, that will keep it steady and make sure that it is your best Jameson.' I reminded him of the conditions of sale as again he was asking for something that was very expensive. Once again, he told me that it wasn't a problem. 'And while you are at it, give me ten of the best Cuban cigars you have in the house,' he said. When he came back into the bar, he looked around the bar and asked the people who were there if they would join him for a drink, and all agreed. While I was packing the bottles, I decided to put in a couple of brandy glasses as it would not do to drink Louis XIII out of the bottle. He was delighted with this. I asked him when he was going to Kerry and he told me he was going that night, so I asked if I could get him a taxi. I rang Shay Cully the local taxi man who made a deal with him and took him to Kerry that night. The whole scenario reminded me of the movie *Cocktail* starring Tom Cruise.

The Budweiser Derby

Back in the early 1990s, Fleishman, Hillard and Saunders was the PR company for the Shelbourne. As it was also the PR company for Budweiser, it put up a lot of its celebrity clients in the hotel.

It was decided one year that a replica Horseshoe Bar would be erected in the VIP marquee in the Curragh, with Sean, George and Elizabeth from the Lounge manning the bar. It was a fantastic day filled with sunshine and celebrities. Everyone enjoyed it and it was a great success.

One of Budweiser's top promoters in those days was a chap called Paul J. Siemer. He was one of those larger-than-life characters. He was staying in the Shelbourne on the weekend that the Tour de France started from Dublin in 1998. He noticed a sign on the counter warning of the traffic disruption that the event was expected to cause. He asked if he could take this sign with him when we had finished with it. I agreed and he took it straight back to his local bar, The Three Dogs, in St Louis, USA. While having a Bud, he slipped the sign onto the bar counter and watched for the reaction of the locals.

A lot of the locals were amazed to hear that the Tour de France was starting in St Louis. After explaining to them that this was not, in fact, the case, he was then able to relate the entire story of his recent trip to include the consumption of an entire bottle of bubbly in his bedroom and the theft of the public notice from the Horseshoe Bar. It seemed that this character always returned from Ireland with crazy stories. I received a letter from Mr Siemer telling me that 'for better or for worse I was now one of them' – he also told me that he would be back Sadly, though, I never saw Mr Siemer again.

Denis O'Brien and the Mobile Phones

Denis O'Brien was more a customer of the Lounge than the Horseshoe Bar. He would hold many a business meeting there when he was researching the mobile phone business in the early 1980s. I think he had quite a battle on his hands as, back in those days, most people could not see a future for mobiles, let alone afford one. They were big, ugly, plastic things resembling a brick. I do remember him one day saying that not that far into the future, children as young as ten would have mobiles. Ironically, all those in his company had laughed at this statement. The joke was soon on them.

Tim Bird

Tim Bird was the bane of my life. He would sit at the bar and desperately look around for someone to talk to, noticing this I would warn him 'no messing' to which he would reply, 'Would I do that?' If I took my eye off him for one second, he would have some unfortunate cornered. The strange thing was that the bullshit he was giving them was fairly believable.

A lady came into the bar one day and asked for me. She told me that an envelope had been left in the bar for her from Tim Bird. I was very suspicious of this. I had a feeling that there was a story of some sort involved, so I asked her about it. She told me that he was a roadie with U2 and that he was to leave her a pair of tickets to their gig in the RDS that weekend. I told her I was so very sorry but no tickets had been left for her.

When Tim came into the hotel, he would go around all of the flower displays taking flowers from them. He would then enter the bar with a bunch of flowers bellowing, 'Where is my birthday girl tonight?' When there was no response, he would make a beeline to the first lady he set his eyes on, get down on one knee, present her with the flowers and declare his undying lover for her. It would not bother him in the least if she was in the company of another man. This was Tim, impulsive and unpredictable. To this very day, he is up to the same antics. Thank God I am no longer in the Horseshoe. Although he is a harmless poor divil, I do feel for the current staff charged with keeping him in order.

The Lotto Winner

In the early days of the National Lottery, the winners were put up in the Shelbourne Hotel. One of the most memorable winners was a young lady from rural Ireland. It was around Christmas time and her whole family were staying in the Shelbourne that weekend. They were a lovely group of people but seemed rather out of their depth in their surroundings. The were dining in No. 27, the main restaurant, and one of the party looked at the table and could not figure out what all of the cutlery was for. Rose, a great Dublin character, was their waitress for the evening. Noting their confusion, she nudged him and said, 'Don't worry about it, I'll keep you right.' When ordering the wine, she was told to get the most expensive as it would be the best. Rose said that while the evening was entertaining, it was a bit of a fiasco.

Brown Thomas had a New Year's sale on at that time and had two fur coats in the window. They were available at a knock-down price – first come, first served.

The lotto winner and her friend queued outside Brown Thomas at 3 a.m. for the coats. Later that day, she sent someone down to Hector Greys for twenty watches, which she gave out to her family and friends amid much pomp and circumstance. Her poor unfortunate boyfriend was heading into the Horseshoe Bar when we heard a roar, 'You're not going in there', at which he turned and walked away.

Another Lotto Winner

One Monday at about 9.30 a.m., a gentleman walked in to the bar. I informed him that we were not yet open. He told me that he just needed a quiet place to sit to get his head together and then said that he had just discovered that he might have won the lotto.

He told me that he was on the bus on his way into town to pay a visit to his building society about his mortgage arrears when he overheard someone talking about the winning numbers. The numbers sounded very familiar – he did the same ones every week. When he got off the bus, he called his wife, told her that he was in the Shelbourne and asked that she bring in an envelope that was on the mantelpiece at home as it was very important. He asked me for a drink to steady his nerves and, again, I told him that I couldn't as we were not open.

At this point, he was pacing up and down the bar and was beginning to annoy me. He kept muttering to himself, 'I've won the lotto. I've won the lotto.' Sometime later, his wife arrived with two children and his elderly mother in tow. When he checked the numbers, he was, indeed, the winner. There were great celebrations. He asked me for a bottle of champagne and some minerals for the kids, I told him I would serve it in the Lounge as that was open. I gave him the bill and he told me that he would fix it up with me later. I was less than happy about this. I had to keep a constant eye on them in case they left without paying. He eventually paid the bill saying neither thank you nor leaving a tip!

The Man up in Jackson's Hole

I got a phone call one evening from a customer and great friend of mine, Frank O'Kane. He was looking for the phone number of a chap in America and was wondering if I could help as the man was known to frequent the Horseshoe from time to time. I said I'd see what I could do. I thought for a moment and realised there were only two people who could possibly know. One was James Craig and the other Arthur McCoy.

I called Arthur and he said that the last he heard of him, the man was in the Bay area of San Francisco but was unsure of his number. He said, 'Ask James Craig, he will surely have it.' I asked James the next day and he said, 'Dear boy, I just might have that number.' He took out his tattered, dog-eared notebook held together by a few elastic bands. After a few minutes of thumbing his way through the pages, he struck gold. We decided to give the number a quick ring to see if the man was there. When the phone was answered, James asked about the man's whereabouts and we were informed that he had an unfortunate incident with an ex-wife whose name we did not know and he had moved to a place called Jackson's Hole. I called Frank back later that day and his wife, Rosaleen, answered the phone. I said, 'Don't take this the wrong way, but the person that Frank is looking for is in Jackson's Hole', and then gave her the phone number he was looking for.

A Black Bush

One Sunday afternoon, two tall, immaculately dressed gentlemen came into the bar and walked around rather nervously. They said they wanted to reserve the far side of the bar and, as there was no one else there but myself and the two of them, I could see no problem with their request. In the space of about fifteen minutes, six more of these guys and an elderly gentleman entered the bar. The six gentlemen stood at certain points of the bar and the elderly gentleman came and stood at the bar. He introduced himself as McCarthy, the American ambassador to Ireland. I introduced myself as Sean, the head bar manager, and welcomed him to the Horseshoe Bar. He asked me what I would recommend for him to drink so I suggested a Black Bush. He stepped back, looked at me quizzically and asked if this was any reflection on his president. I assured him it was not. I explained to him that Black Bush was a fine Irish liquor whiskey of great character! I understand the story was later told in the White House to great amusement.

Ambassador Richard Ryan

Ambassador Richard Ryan when back in town from one of his many overseas postings always paid me a visit. The first drink of Gordon's and tonic was always on me. When pleasantries were over, he would ask where his friends were to be found. These were the days before mobile phones ruled our lives. If it was at lunch-time, I would know immediately where they were dining. It would often be Dobbin's, Brown's or La Mère Zou. Ambassador Ryan had served in many countries around including South Korea, Spain, the Netherlands and as ambassador to UN, where he negotiated Ireland's place on the Security Council. He also played a major role representing Ireland's interests in London where it was said of him that he was 'the man who dined for Ireland'. A most congenial clubman and a member of London's Garrick and Dublin's Kildare Street and University clubs where he entertained in great style. He is also a published poet who counts among his friends, a generation of poets produced by Northern Ireland, including Seamus Heaney, Derek Mahon and John Montague.

The Man Who Worked at the Abbey Theatre

There was a chap who used to drink in the Horseshoe in my early days – unfortunately I can't remember his name. He played some part in the functioning of the Abbey Theatre during the time in which Noel Pearson was the artistic director. When he had had a few drinks, this fellow would become a bit of a nuisance. I had to speak to him on numerous occasions. Things got to the point where I was going to bar him. When I told him this, he became very upset. He told me that if he was refused service, he could lose his job. I asked him how this could possibly be. He said that Noel Pearson was his boss and if he was not allowed to have a drink in here, it would be very bad for his reputation. He pleaded with me and promised that there would be no more trouble. I explained to him that I had already warned him several times. I watched him as he went over to Noel and spoke with him for some time. He came back to me and asked if I would change my mind if he behaved himself from then on. (I had already changed my mind.) How mighty was the power of the Horseshoe!

John O'Byrne: The Wee Man with the Big Cigar

John O'Byrne was a regular of the Horseshoe and a friend of mine for many years. He was one of Ireland's greatest restaurateurs and Dobbin's was his kingdom. John was small in stature but larger than life with a personality and presence that would fill any room, but he was no angel and could be quite difficult at times. One evening, he arrived in the Horseshoe, a little under the weather, with one of his friends. During the course of the evening, he became quite loud and boisterous, so much so that I had to have a word with him and ask him to watch his language. I was keeping a constant eye on the situation. He was getting out of hand, so I went out from behind the counter and called him aside, saying, 'If I were to behave in Dobbin's the way you are behaving here what would you do about it?' He said to me 'point taken' and apologised.

Monday Lunch

It was customary for several of John O'Byrne's friends to have lunch – which would run into the evening – in Dobbin's every Monday. In the party would be Frank O'Kane, Noel Pearson, Pat Cousins, Jerry O'Connor, Michael Rogers and one or two more. When John had eaten his fill, he would suggest retiring to the Horseshoe Bar and would order a couple of taxis. He would then send his friends ahead and follow shortly after. When John arrived, he would pick out a nice red wine from the list and when the wine arrived, it would be presented for tasting. John would look at the wine, study it, taste it and would then look at me. By the look he gave me, I always knew what was coming next. 'This wine is corked. What sort of a cellar have you got?' I would hurry off to retrieve another bottle and, again, present it and wait. He would look at me again as if studying me for my reaction and say, 'Not great but I suppose it will do.' Over the course of the evening, he would drink a few bottles and smoke his usual cigar, a large Havana. Towards the end of the evening, John would call for another bottle for the road. I would bring out the very first bottle that he had said was corked, present it, let him taste it and await his reaction. He would look at me smile, give a wink and say, 'It's fine.' We both knew that he had been testing me from the very start. This was what made him such a magical character who is so sadly missed.

The Birthday Party

In 1999, the Shelbourne celebrated its 175th birthday and a formal bash was organised to mark this special occasion. Unfortunately, it was impossible to invite everyone. We in the Horseshoe were asked to give a list of twenty names. I gave in a list of 200 – counting partners, it increased to 400 – and it was returned to me to count out twenty. I managed to cut the list and retuned it. Shortly after, I was bombarded with customers looking for the reason that they were not invited. I had to say that the ballroom only held so many but told them to come along and I would look after them on the night.

Sean's parents, John and Pauline Boyd, in Cashal, Carrick on Shannon, 1935.

Tommy, Sean and Cecilia Boyd with Margaret Murray at their First Holy Communion, St Malachy's Church in Belfast, 1950.

(Above) Sean outside the Old Harbour Bar, formerly the Harbour Lights Bar, fifty years after he began his apprenticeship there.

(Left) Sean's uncle, John Brennan, with Sean and his sister Cecilia, 1959. John ran the Harbour Lights Bar just off James Street.

These are the canal men with whom I travelled from Dublin to Carrick-on-Shannon on the 52m boat.

Sean posing proudly with his first car, a Hillman Husky Estate, Belfast, 1967.

Sean receives the trophy for winning the all-Ireland Bisque de Bush cocktail competition, 1967.

Sean celebrates his win with friends in Belfast, 1967.

Sean with members of Bartenders Guild of Northern Ireland after his win, 1967.

(Above) Sean serving the last drink in the Hibernian Hotel to Sean Dunne, 1981.

(Right) Sean pulling his first official pint of Guinness in Forte Grand in Abu Dhabi, 1994.

Sean with his daughter Etain, his wife Josephine and his son Daragh at the first birthday party of Etain's beauty salon, Urban Beauty.

On the big night, I got myself the job of collecting the invitations on the door and I managed to pass in many of my regulars. When I was on the door, I got the news that John O'Byrne had suffered a stroke while dressing for the party, which took the shine off the evening. I was anxious to hear how he was as were many of his friends who were thinking of him. It took some time for John to recover, but recover he did. It was marvellous to see him back and full of mischief.

As time rolled on, John visited on several occasions, sometimes having a drink or two. One night, he arrived in with some of his friends and, over the course of the evening, he asked me for a light for his cigar. I looked at him in disbelief and said, 'You want me to give a light for you cigar?'

He said, 'Yes.'

I said, 'No, no, no.'

He then shouted over to Noel Pearson and kept going on about the fact that I wouldn't give him a light. Noel Pearson said, 'Give him a light, for God's sake.'

I said to both of them that a year earlier I had been lighting candles for John, so I certainly was not lighting a cigar now. They both had no answer to this.

Unfortunately, sometime later, John had another stroke from which he never recovered. Dobbin's is still as good as ever, under the stewardship of Pat Walsh. John and Dobbin's will always survive.

The Traveller Wedding

It was always customary in Banqucting for event sheets to be out a week in advance. One afternoon, Paddy Murphy, the head waiter, was going through the sheets in the Lock Up. He took one sheet out and said, 'This wedding is a Traveller wedding.' This was brought to the attention of the banqueting manager who immediately called in the person who took the booking to find out if this was true. The wedding had been booked only ten days beforehand and paid for in full, in cash. This was the talk of the hotel as none of us knew what to expect. The wedding was booked for a Saturday morning.

I was standing in the front hall speaking with one of our staff members when a large, blue furniture van drew up outside the front door. They let the tail board-down and out poured the guests for the wedding. There were about fifteen or twenty boys no older than ten years of age all dressed in morning suits and top hats. They invaded the Lobby, with the rest of the guests following behind, and completely took over the Lord Mayor's Lounge and the Horseshoe Bar. The only two people on duty in Horseshoe Bar were Charlie Brady and myself.

The guests were screaming at us for a drink. Charlie said, 'I'm out of here.'

'You stay where you are,' I said.

I asked how they proposed to pay for the drinks and who was in charge of the party. A man came forward and told me that he was the bride's uncle and that he would be handling the bill. We, eventually, got them all served but I had to keep an eye on the uncle to make sure that he didn't disappear. They were called to the wedding reception in the Ballroom, where they were to have tea, coffee, sandwiches and drinks before going elsewhere for a meal later in the evening.

When they had eventually left the Horseshoe, I lost sight of the uncle and had quite a job tracking him down. When I found him in the Ballroom, I approached him with the bill. He took a look at it and laughed at me saying, 'I ordered no drinks for them, I'll pay for my own and they can pay for their own.'

I reminded him that he had said he was covering the bill and told him I was not leaving until I was paid. I could tell by the uncle's attitude that he had no intention of paying. I then looked around for the father of the bride and approached him. I told him of the dilemma regarding the drinks and that I expected that as they had been ordered, they would be paid for. The bride's father, who seemed to be a bit of a character, put his hand in his pocket, took out a wad of notes, paid the bill, apologised to me and said he would have a quiet word with the uncle later.

I returned to the Horseshoe where Charlie was fit to be tied. 'Did you get paid?'

'Of course I got paid,' I said. I told him that the bride's father was a perfect gentleman and had covered the bill.

The little gentlemen in the top hats were still invading the Lounge and the Lobby. They were everywhere. They were lifting everything in sight and we had to chase them to retrieve the hotel's property. When it was time for them to leave, the whole hotel went out to see the bride off. The guests in the house were fascinated by the whole idea and thought it was fantastic. A Hiace van drew up outside the Ballroom door, the bride and groom got in and the bride leaned out of the window and threw her bouquet to the bridesmaids on the steps. Then they drove off up Merrion Row to cheers of delight from the guests.

The Man with the Rabbit

One Saturday afternoon, Charlie Brady was on duty when in walked a gentleman wearing a long raincoat. He walked up and down the bar as if looking for someone. Charlie thought he looked a bit strange and was wary of him. The man approached the bar, opened his coat, put his hand inside, took out a rabbit and put it on the counter. The rabbit sat on the counter sniffing the air looking at Charlie who, for once, was lost for words. Charlie looked at the man, who just reached down, picked up the rabbit, put it in his pocket and walked out the door. The story is testament to the fact that anything could and *did* happen in the Horseshoe Bar.

Michael J., the Prince of Donegal

Michael J. O'Doherty was known to only the select few of us as Michael Duvet. He hailed from Donegal and was an entrepreneur who was involved in backpacker's accommodation in both Dublin and Donegal. One time, Michael was opening a hostel in Donegal and had invited several of his friends up for the occasion. While there, they would take in a golfing trip. He reminded his friends that, as it was the month of March, they were to take their duvets with them, hence the name Michael Duvet.

Michael had the reputation of being a bit of a snob. One evening during their trip, a friend of his opened the bonnet of his Jeep outside the local pub to explain to another friend the type of engine it had. Michael came out saying, 'Close that bonnet! The only time you open the bonnet in Donegal is when you are in trouble!'

The Civil Servants

One evening, two gentlemen and a lady arrived in to the bar. The lady was in a very intoxicated state and kept slipping off her stool. I said to the gentleman, 'I'm sorry, I cannot serve this lady.'

The gentleman got very upset and told me that she was fine and that they would look after her. I insisted that I was not serving her as she had had enough to drink. They demanded to speak to the manager. I told them, 'You are speaking to him.'

Still unhappy, they went to Reception to make an official complaint. The duty manager that night was Maebh Breathnach, who was our HR manager. She spoke with the gentleman and rang me in the bar to say they were okay and that I was to serve them. I refused. The trio left the bar under protest, assuring me that I would hear from them again.

A few days later, I was called to the food and beverage manager's office and handed a letter of complaint that had just arrived. I read the letter and told my boss that I would handle it. I had noted that the complaint was written on Oireachtas-headed paper from the Department of Education.

I rang the telephone number on the right-hand corner and asked to speak with the civil servant in question. I told him that I had received his letter and asked him what right he had to make a complaint about me using taxpayers' money. I told him that, as a taxpayer, I took great exception to this. The phone went down and that was the end of the conversation.

Richard Harris

I met Richard Harris on many occasions during my time in the Shelbourne. My earliest memory of him was in the old Grill Bar one afternoon. In his right hand, he was holding, very tightly, a bottle of Evian water. While he was waiting for his meal to be served, he called me over and said, 'A guy is gonna come though that door in the next few minutes, he will be wearing clothes held together with safety pins, and will have a safety pin in his nose and his ear. If he comes near me, you are to tell him to leave as I am not to be disturbed.'

Sure enough, a few moments later, a guy walked through the door with dyed blond hair and safety pins everywhere. I went to him and told him that Mr Harris was not to be disturbed. The man replied, 'Da, don't be like that.' That was my first encounter with Richard Harris and his son.

A good many years later, Richard was in the Horseshoe Bar. He was on his way to Limerick to the funeral of his brother-in-law and was still holding on tight to a bottle of Evian. Richard had been off the drink for many years and trusted nothing but his bottle of Evian. There were quite a few others in the bar that morning also going to the funeral. Amongst them were Daragh O'Malley and Arthur McCoy.

A few days later, Richard was back in the Horseshoe and I was talking to him about the funeral. He suddenly looked up at me and said, 'I'll have a glass of Guinness.' I was rather taken aback at this. I pulled him a glass of Guinness, placed it in front of him and asked him when he had started to drink again. He told me that while at the funeral, he was looking at the family burial plot and thought to himself, All these guys in there, what they would not give for a glass of Guinness and here am I depriving myself of that very thing. 'It was then that I decided I was going to have a glass of Guinness,' he said.

On the way back from the funeral, the other two characters, O'Malley and McCoy, were passing through Nenagh when they were stopped by the gardaí for speeding. The garda asked if they had been drinking. They said that they were returning from a funeral. The garda said, 'I didn't ask you that, I asked if you had been drinking.' What happened next was never really clear but the two boys arrived back in Dublin safe and sound.

Peter O'Toole

Peter O'Toole is famous for many things – *Lawrence of Arabia, Goodbye, Mr Chips* and a host of other films. In the Shelbourne, he is famous for one thing – having a bath in champagne!

He loved the old hotel and was a regular guest. Whenever he stayed, he always asked to be looked after by John Melia who was the only man who could charm him. To get him up for breakfast, John had a great trick. He would enter the room and say, 'Now, Mr O'Toole, you're needed on set.' When he didn't respond, John would roll up the end of the bedcovers and tickle his toes until the great actor could resist no longer!

The Bar Tab

When I took over the Horseshoe Bar in 1989, there was quite a number of tabs still in the book. Bar tabs were illegal and frowned upon by management, so I decided that these tabs had to go. Everything was running very smoothly for a while, with no problems.

As time passed, we would find that there was one or two people who had a tab. They would run up a few drinks and leave without paying so that we had to chase them for the bill the next time they came in. When anyone started a tab who was not a regular, it was common practice to ask for a credit card.

One afternoon, I was called to the general manager's office over a complaint that had been made about my refusal to run a tab. I informed that manager that I didn't run tabs unless payment was being made by credit card. He then informed me that two or three people had permanent tabs. I replied that this was not true, that any drinks left unpaid had to be signed off at close of business that evening. I explained to him that some people might have the wrong idea about certain customers having a tab as these customers had an account with the company and so they never actually signed off the tab at the end of the evening, they trusted me to to do this for them.

What never ceased to amaze me was the number of credit cards left behind on an average evening. Some went unclaimed for weeks. Often, I had to try to find the owners to give them their cards back.

Daragh O'Malley

I met Daragh O'Malley, who came from the distinguished Limerick political dynasty, when I first took over the Horseshoe. In those days, he was an actor of sorts but was also a theatrical agent – though I think he spent as much time in the Horseshoe as he did in his office. He is a man with a wonderful sense of humour. His drink in those days was a Mickey O'Rourke special – a large vodka and a sparkling Ballygowan. You took two twenty-ounce slim jims filled with ice, put a large vodka in one glass, then filled the glass with Ballygowan and then continue to add the ice from the other glass into the Ballygowan. He certainly did know how to drink them. When someone joined his company, he would always insist on ordering a margarita for them. He said that I made the best one in Dublin with a twinkle and a sparkle in his eye.

The Betting Docket

One day, Daragh O'Malley arrived in as usual. He asked me to hold a betting docket for him and explained that he had done a double bet of a £1,000 on the winner of Wimbledon and for Germany to win the 1990 World Cup. He had spoken with Eamon Dunphy who had indicated that Germany would win. He asked me to hold on to his betting slip as he had a habit of losing them. I pinned the docket on to the wall of my locker and thought no more of it.

The first part of the bet came up and he was very excited about it. I was on holiday when the World Cup was on. When I arrived back to the Horseshoe, I was told that Daragh was looking for me. He had gone to management and said that I had placed an envelope in the safe, they had looked for it but none could be found. On hearing this, I telephoned Daragh and, as usual, got his answering machine and had to leave a message. 'Daragh, this is Sean. I am sitting outside a little café on the Champs Elysées in Paris. I have a bottle of DP with two glasses, hurry the ice is melting.'

Daragh walked into the Horseshoe and stopped dead in his tracks when he saw me. He shouted at me, 'Where's my docket?'

I said, 'You gave it to me to hold and that is what I did. All you had to do is wait till I got back and not involve the management.' I went down to my locker, took the envelope from the wall and gave it to him. He told me that the docket was worth a lot of money. Sometime later, Daragh took acting more seriously. He married the beautiful Gabriel and moved to Los Angles where he did very well for himself. They had two additions to the family, his beloved dog Paddy and his parrot, who spent all day watching MTV.

Daragh worked with Sean Bean on the *Sharpe* television series, which was set during the Spanish–French wars. He played the part of a northern Irish man called Sergeant Harper. He also worked on a film in Cork with Marlon Brando with whom he became great friends. The film turned into a financial problem where no one was paid but Brando. When Daragh asked him how he managed to get his money, Brando said, 'Get paid first, work later.' It was said that he was paid a million punts up front.

Down and Out in London

One wet night, Daragh O'Malley was filming on location in London. He was playing the part of an Irish boxer down on his luck and sleeping rough. A guy who had once worked in the Horseshoe Bar passed him and recognised him. He said, 'Is that you, Daragh?' There was no answer. 'It's Padraig. Don't you know me? I used to work in the Horseshoe.' Daragh told him to go away and Padraig said, 'You're coming home with me, things can't be that bad.'

   All of a sudden, a lot of people appeared from nowhere and asked Daragh if he was all right. Daragh told them all he was fine, turned to Padraig and told him that he was on location and that there were cameras across the road. Everyone was very amused at what had happened. Daragh tells this story with great pride as one of our own would never leave a fellow Irishman down and out on the streets of London. Daragh and Gabriel are back in Ireland and doing very well living down in County Meath. Sadly, poor Paddy has passed on, but the parrot is still watching MTV.

Wanderly Wagon

Virginia Cole is another great lady whom I loved to see coming in. She had a great smile and always had a warm welcome for me. She is a true member of the Arts and a great actress. I remember one day introducing my daughter, Etain, to her. Etain said, 'I remember you; I fell out of my pram watching you on *Wanderly Wagon*.' At one time, Virginia was married to John McColgan of *Riverdance* fame and their daughter, Lucy McColgan, also became a Horseshoe regular.

The Returned Yank

Griffin Healy arrived in Dublin in the month of August for the Rose of Tralee festival. Bord Fáilte booked him in to the Shelbourne with strict instruction of bed and board only – he was to pay for all of his own food and bar bills. He arrived into the Horseshoe speaking in a stage-Irish Hollywood accent and cried out, 'Aw begorrah, Seanín, I'm back.' This guy was larger than life. His drink was a pint glass filled to the top with ice, with a large J&B scotch and then filled to the top with water. He would hold on to the glass and as people bought him a drink he would add it to the glass. He didn't buy much but always drank plenty. James Craig, an old friend of Griffin's, always loved to see him coming in.

Griffin is a big guy with a moustache that reminded you of a walrus. With this, and his stage-Irish accent, he was always a big hit with the ladies. When the festival was over, he returned to Dublin generally with a female companion. He booked into the hotel and his mother back in Chicago picked up the tab – she would cover him for a week or two but, of course, Griffin would always overstay his welcome. When the bill was returned unpaid and his mother would not answer the calls, Griffin was in trouble. This never seemed to bother him and he just kept the façade going for as long as possible.

He always knew when the girls at Reception had a letter for him asking him to pay his bill or leave. He would arrive late in the evening, knowing that management would not be on duty, and would be laden down with bunches of flowers for the girls and say, 'Beautiful cailíns of Ireland, I lay my heart on the desk before you', and with all of the charm he could muster, he would melt their hearts and, of course, the eviction notice was overlooked. Things always ended well and his mother always paid the bill so that he could go home. Griffin Healy is still out there charming the ladies.

The Flying Doctor

This man was the greatest bullshitter I have ever met. He was, I believe, a salesman of sorts. He would worm his way into the company of a group of ladies and introduce himself as a pilot – at other times he would introduce himself as a doctor, which is how he got the nickname, the Flying Doctor. To be fair, he seemed to have had a fair bit of knowledge on the subject. Maybe, though, this was just because those around him knew less than he did. He would get great mileage out of this. Having introduced himself as a doctor he would diagnose people's complaints. His luck ran out one day when Dr Mc was in the bar having his usual bottle of Bulmer's and witnessed him giving out what he believed were prescriptions. He challenged him, and the Flying Doctor left very quickly.

I had not seen him for sometime when, one day, he arrived in and proceeded with his customary bullshitting. He got into conversation with a customer who had been very ill and asked him about his illness. I overheard him saying, 'I think they diagnosed you wrongly', and he then went on to give the customer his opinion and told him to see a friend of his in Blackrock Clinic. Upon hearing this, I had to pull him aside and ask him to go before I had him removed. The Flying Doctor went to the toilet and did not return.

That evening, the man and his wife returned to the bar asking for him. I told them that he was not a doctor and they were not to believe anything he had said. The wife wanted his name so that she could have him prosecuted as a fraud.

Patrick Cassidy

Patrick Cassidy worked on many movie themes and travelled between Ireland and the US. His brother, Frank, is his agent. When they were in Dublin, they were regulars at the Horseshoe. Patrick's passion was to compose 'The Children of Lir' which was first performed in Dublin. He has been hailed as the Seán Ó Riada of his generation and, together with Frank, has done brilliantly in LA.

Paul Bisset

Well-known businessman, Paul Bisset was another regular. He drove a Rolls Royce to the door so you always knew when he was about the hotel. When I took over the Horseshoe, he was reported to have said, 'Now we don't have to go to Doheny & Nesbitts for our second drink, we can get one here.'

Patrick Gallagher

Patrick was the one-time boss of the Gallagher Building Group. On the morning of his release from Maghaberry Prison, his first stop was the Horseshoe Bar for a pint with his wife. James Craig was sitting at the bar and, on seeing Patrick, welcomed him home and joined them for a drink. After all of the pleasantries were over, James approached the bar and asked if I would change a cheque for Patrick. I thought for a moment and said I would. Patrick said to me, 'Hold on to this cheque, for it will be worth money some day. My first cheque after my release.' Needless to say, I didn't hold on to the cheque and it was honoured. Gallagher went from being a multimillionaire to being broke and imprisoned. He was pre-Celtic Tiger, his father having made the family fortune, and had been a rich man in a very poor country. Despite his difficulties, Patrick remained a gentleman. It is said that his written but unpublished memoirs contain riveting stories of his dealings with Haughey and other personalities of the era.

The Lady who Wanted to Make a Phone Call

I first met Geraldine Mahon, wife of John Mahon, the famous New York publican, one afternoon when I was at Reception waiting to collect change. I heard a lady ask if she could make a phone call. The receptionist asked if she was a resident to which she replied, 'No, I'm sorry.' Geraldine was upset when she was told that, as a non-resident, she could not use the phone. I tapped her on the shoulder and told her to follow me. I let her use the phone in the Horseshoe and she was very grateful. To me, it was nice to help a damsel in distress. It was then that she told me her name was Geraldine Mahon. Later in the week, she returned with some friends and her mother, who was a very beautiful woman. She said to her companions, 'This is the man who came to my aid in my hour of need.' We have remained friends ever since.

Dessie Hynes

Dessie Hynes was a Longford man of great renown. He had a great way with words and was a very humorous man. In the 1990s, he owned O'Donoghue's pub in Merrion Row, which, under his ownership, continued to be a famous venue for Irish music. It was here that The Dubliners started their career. You would find him with Senator Maurice Manning, Gary Hart (the one-time Democratic candidate) and Senator Edward Kennedy. He was also a great friend of most of the Irish rugby players of that era.

Eddie Linden

In 1969, when he was still in London, Eddie Linden founded *Aquarius* magazine. He is also a poet. He always arrived at the Horseshoe in August, on his way to the Humbert Summer School in Ballina, County Mayo. (I am also a member of this school.)

Eddie sat at the bar and talked incessantly. He was born in the North and was very proud of his roots – this was the only thing we had in common. One day, he was sitting at the bar with John Moran. I was not paying him much heed.

Feeling ignored, he called me over and said, 'Do you know I am gay?' I said nothing. Once again he said, 'I'm gay.' I looked at him and said, 'What do you want me to do about it?' His reply was, 'I'm only saying.' How odd, the life of the confessional.

The Two Regulars

Two regulars on Wednesday and Saturday nights were Patrick Howard and Martin Fennely – two of the nicest characters I ever had the pleasure of serving. Patrick was a very successful fashion designer and gave it all up to open an antique shop in Francis Street. Martin gave up his job as a bank manager to do the same. Patrick is the brother of the legendary chef, John Howard, who was proprietor of Le Coq Hardi, in its day, the most famous restaurant in Ireland. It was there the Charlie Haughey and Terry Keane conducted their famous love affair.

Complaints

One day, I was asked by a customer how I would handle a complaint. I said, 'I would listen.' I always keep in mind this famous quotation from Samuel Johnston, 'Many a man would rather you heard his story than solve his problem.' Back to the old confessional again.

The Shipyard – Harland and Wolff

Pat Doherty, one of Ireland's leading developers, had many developments throughout the world. He was famous for many things, amongst them being painted several times by Lucien Freud. He was also a regular in the Horseshoe Bar.

He often came in with a few of his friends for his favourite tipple, a glass of champagne. One day, he arrived in on his own, which was unusual. He sat up at the bar and said, 'Sean, I just bought the shipyard.'

I thought for a moment and said, 'You mean Harland and Wolff?'

'Yes,' came the answer.

I said, 'What in the name of God are you going to do with it?'

He told me of his vision of apartments, houses, shops cinemas, parks and a marina. On the main thoroughfare, known as Titanic Way, he envisaged a hotel which would be a replica of the *Titanic* herself. He was very excited about the project and I jokingly asked him to put one by for me. He said, 'Sean, I remember going there for a job and I couldn't even get though the gate.' How things have changed, a little guy from Derry now owned the shipyard that refused him a job.

A Little Gem

I was on duty one afternoon when two young ladies came into the bar. One was very familiar but I couldn't place her – I thought she was very young and so I would have to refuse her. She had a fantastic smile. She asked for two large bottles of mineral water for her room. As soon as she spoke, I knew who she was. It was Kylie Minogue. She was so small, she stood on the foot rail, leaned over the counter and smiled. I asked her for her room number and, at that, the two left the bar, laughing. I think she wasn't sure if I recognised her or not. Nor did it matter to her or to me.

Greed

The Horseshoe Bar was a very popular bar with champagne drinkers. Between 1998 and 2000, we had the largest sales of champagne in Ireland. Our main sellers were Veuve Clicquot and Nicolas Feuillatte and I had built up a very good champagne trade during this period of time.

One day, I received a memo advising me that a review of prices was to be held that afternoon and the price of champagne was on the agenda. A rise of £10 a bottle was proposed by Richard Margo, the food and beverage manager. I bitterly opposed this but was overruled.

The food and beverage manager said, 'These people have loads of money and it's up to us to get it.' I went to Jean Ricoux, the manager, and explained to him that this price hike would kill the business, he said that the food and beverage manager had the right to make this decision.

When asked to describe the Shelbourne, this same manager said it was a 'big bar'. To me, he had very little regard for the hotel and its people. For instance, on the day of the 9/11 disaster, when all premises closed in Dublin, he kept the bars in the Shelbourne open – greed on top of greed.

Jim Hand

One Saturday morning, I was having breakfast listening to Eamon Dunphy interview Paddy Cole. I knew Paddy well as he used to call into the bar every now and again. I heard them mention Jim Hand, a showbusiness impressario of the Albert era. I only really knew Jim in his latter days, and he was a sad sight to behold. He used to come in to the bar and apologise for his attire, saying that he had sat with princes, great stars and celebrities of the day, and now he was apologising to me. I would sit him down and make him a mock Irish coffee – an Irish coffee without the whiskey – which he enjoyed very much. I was very fond of him and was very sad when he died.

All-Ireland Tickets

On the eve of an All-Ireland final, it was customary for Oliver Barden to hold court in the Horseshoe with his friends. He usually had a few friends over from the US; he would also have Judge Kilellen and circuit Judge Walsh.

In 1993, the All-Ireland football final was between Derry and Cork. Oliver was short two tickets and asked if I could do anything for him. As it happened, Derry man, Kevin Kelly, publisher of several magazines, including *Food and Wine* and founder of *The World of Interiors*, was hosting a dinner in Room 112, the Constitution Room. One of his guests was a famous all-Ireland Cavan winner from the 1940s called Des Benson. I approached Des and told him of my predicament and he got me two tickets free of charge. I retuned to the bar and gave them to Oliver, who put the two tickets in his top pocket, and told hold him there was no charge. Oliver was delighted with this. Derry won that All-Ireland for the first time and the team had their victory dinner in the Ballroom of the Shelbourne.

Later that evening, Oliver arrived in as usual and I asked him how he enjoyed the match. He said, 'All my friends enjoyed the match, but I wasn't there as I couldn't get a ticket.' I looked at him, reached over, put my hand into his pocket and took out the two tickets. He looked at me with astonishment and disbelief. I told Des and he was not amused. After that, he would always say to me coming up to an all-Ireland, 'Don't even think of asking me for a ticket.'

Oliver Caffrey and 'the Soul of Ireland'

One evening, an American man arrived into the Horseshoe, looked around him and was overheard saying, 'What's so different about this place?'

Oliver Caffrey, a long-time patron of the Horseshoe, was standing beside him. Looking around to see who had made the remark, Oliver replied, 'This bar is the soul of Ireland.'

The man told him that he was instructed to visit the bar if he was ever in Ireland and was still wondering what was so special about it.

Oliver said, 'What other bar in the world has two people in it who could call the White House and have the president accept their call?'

The Yank protested that this was impossible as there was protocol to follow. He asked who Oliver was talking about and Oliver replied, 'Besides myself, there is also John Hume and, in the corner over there, sits Bono.'

I must add that Bill Clinton was the president at the time, but I am sure this would still be the case today.

Oliver and Maureen Nulty

Oliver and Maureen Nulty were owners of the Oriel Gallery in Clare Street, just across the road from where Samuel Beckett's father had had his office. Oliver was immensely stylish, always dressed in the finest, bespoke tailoring and generous to a fault. He discovered and promoted the work of the painter Markey Robinson and when many disparaged it, he saw its worth. It was Oliver who also created confidence in the Irish art market by giving a guarantee to patrons of his gallery to buy back at cost any picture purchased. Oliver was a great supporter of the United Arts Club, an institution founded by Yeats and Sarah Purser, and, when he died, he willed a substantial sum of money to the club for refurbishment purposes. Maureen Nulty was a great supporter and promoter of the Irish couturiers.

Smirnoff

When I took over the Horseshoe, the only vodka on display was Huzzar. I immediately added Smirnoff to the list.

When I first knew Tom Keaveney, he was the boss of Gilbey's of Ireland, he is now chairman of Morgan's wine merchants. Tom was in the bar accompanied by his usual pals, Paddy Madigan, Mick Cuddy and a few others and I heard him say, 'It is easy to see that there is a new man in charge of the Horseshoe.'

'Smirnoff and tonic, please', was the order.

Paul Carthy

Paul Carthy was a frequent visitor to the Horseshoe when he was general manager of Guinness Storehouse. However, he has worked in many hotels in different parts of the world. I met him in Abu Dhabi when I was with Irish tourism. When he was in Singapore, managing the Meridien Changi Hotel on Orchard Road, he did me a good turn by looking after my daughter, Etain, when she was travelling on her own. I will never forget this.

Baileys Whiskey

Christina Forest and John Ryan launched Baileys Whiskey in the Horseshoe in 1997 – on the fortieth birthday of the Horseshoe Bar. Baileys Whiskey had the distinct flavour of caramel and was a very good product – its only downfall was in the name. People always got it mixed up with Bailey's Cream. Later, John Ryan went on to produce a very fine vodka called Boru.

The Three Amigos

The three amigos – Louise Gunn, and Jake and Pat Lennon – would brighten the darkest of a dull day. So to would Tom Healy, former general manager of the Irish Stock Exchange who would speak in Latin to Fr Sean Quigley or anyone else who could respond or understand.

Thee Men from the *Sun*

Ritchie Taylor, at present, writes for the *Evening Herald*. When he was working for the *Sun* in Huguenot House, he and his friends could be found in the Horseshoe for a lunch-time tipple. They were the last guardians of the journalist traditions of Fleet Street. What I miss most about the Horseshoe, is the conversation, along with, of course, its people. Ronan O'Reilly was another of the group along with the unforgettable Myles McEntee. There was a long tradition of journalists drinking there, given the proximity of the hotel to the parliament building and the fact that most of the business done in Dublin in those days was done in the Horseshoe.

The Cartier Million

In the early days of my captaincy of the Horseshoe, Jonathan Irvine was a regular. I remember the excitement when he organised the Cartier Million Horserace at the Phoenix Park racecourse. Sadly, this is no longer running today, because Mick Flynn built houses and apartments where it used to take place.

Charlie Murless

Charlie Murless, well-known and respected in Ireland's bloodstock industry, is one of Ireland's great characters. He married Rhona Blake after a very long romance – I often wondered if they would ever get married at all. Rhona worked for Fleishman, Hillard and Saunders, a major PR company. Today, she is the boss of Fleishman-Hillard – John Saunders became the director of Fleishman-Hillard Communications.

Getting back to Charlie, he managed a racecourse in England, I think it was Doncaster. He told me a great story of a race meeting at Doncaster that was to be graced by the presence of Queen Elizabeth II. There was great excitement about her visit. Protocol was very strict for these visits. The royals even brought toilet seats for the Queen. Charlie thought to himself that he could have thrown a great toilet-seat party but, unfortunately, they were all taken away.

After Charlie and Rhona did finally marry, he became the manager of Punchestown Racecourse in County Kildare. He oversaw the transformation of the racecourse to what it is today. Charlie's favourite drink was a champagne Pimms number one mix.

John Hurt

John Hurt was a great friend and we spent many hours discussing his great film roles. I was his guest at the Dublin première of *Captain Corelli's Mandolin* in which he starred with Penélope Cruz and Nicolas Cage. He talked of his time in Greece and the making of the film, and of the heavy woollen clothes they had worn for the film, which was set during the Second World War. John played a doctor in the film and a wounded Captain Corelli was brought to him for treatment. For the scene, John had worn an earpiece through which he received direction about how to describe the wound and how to operate on it. When he was at a very delicate part of the operation, hand shaking and sweat dripping from his brow, a voice came over the earpiece, 'Where will you be having dinner tonight and who will your guests be?'

When John was on a set, he never drank and when home on leave, he would call in to the Horseshoe and have his customary mock coffee – an Irish coffee without the whiskey. In the history of the Horseshoe, no tea or coffee was served. I believe this has changed now.

John and his then Irish girlfriend were at a fundraising dinner for Paul Newman's Barretstown Camp, which I also attended. I gave my services for auction, the prize being that I would serve cocktails and dinner in the home of the highest bidder. The fundraiser is organised each year by Blaise O'Hara amongst others. John bid €7,000 for the privilege of my services. Unfortunately, he was having his Lough Dan home renovated at the time and the debt is still pending.

John often came in with Gareth Browne and they frequently adjourned to Michael O'Sullivan's nearby flat for drinks before dinner at La Mère Zou. John is now married to Anwen Rees Meyers.

Legal Eagles

A solicitor, whom I have known all my life – I went to school with his brothers – was the son of a Belfast publican, a fine, big man. The family left Belfast in the early 1970s. This guy would come into the Horseshoe on a Friday night and drink his pint of Smitwicks. When paying, he would hand me a lump of loose change and he was always ten or fifteen cent short. By the time, I had counted it, he would have gone from the bar. I bided my time and always got my money.

I saw him driving in Merrion Square one evening and was quite surprised at the state of the car he was driving. When I saw him again, I asked him who owned the car that he had been driving and he said that he did. I went out from behind the counter, put one arm around his shoulder and said, 'My friend, I want you to visualise this, one day whether it be long or short, I do hope it be long, a group of people will be standing where we are now, they will be drinking DP champagne and they will be toasting your memory. They will say wasn't he a great uncle, he never spent a shilling.' Some weeks later, I saw him driving a new Mercedes with a Northern reg. His older brother always maintained this man spelled God with an *l*.

The Man from Pallas Foods

Tadgh Geary was a regular among the young business tycoons who used the Horseshoe Bar as a social and business venue. He hailed from an old respectable business family in County Limerick that established one of the most successful food-distribution companies ever seen in Ireland. Since the early 1980s, the business has evolved into one of the leading food-service distributors on the island of Ireland and the famaous red logo is one of the most visible on the roads of Ireland. Tadgh brought a wide circle of friends to the Horseshoe, many of them from the established business world and many who were on the way up. He was always ready to give a helping hand to someone with a good business idea and is much respected at home and internationally for his business acumen coupled with great charm and wit.

Alan Devlin

Alan Devlin is one of Ireland's great character actors of stage and screen. Unfortunately, he will be most remembered for Noel Pearson's production of the *Pirates of Penzance* in Dublin's Gaiety Theatre when, one night, in the middle of the performance, he walked off of the stage and was heard to say, 'Fuck it, I'm going for a drink', or words to that effect. He was wearing a radio mic and walked with it still on to the nearby Neary's pub.

He paid the occasional visit to the Horseshoe. One evening, he walked in wearing a yellow fireman's hat and jacket, carrying a foghorn and roaring his head off. I do not know how he got past the doorman, but he did. He spotted

Noel Pearson and coming up behind him let off the foghorn in his ear and then danced around the bar laughing his head off. He was mad drunk. How Noel stopped himself from killing him I will never know. We got him out of the bar and I apologised to Noel who replied, 'It's not your fault. What a waste of a great talent.'

Some years later, Alan arrived in to the Horseshoe. I saw him coming and put up my hand and said, 'You are not being served here.' He kept trying to convince me, with arms outstretched and a smile on his face. Only, he had that talent. The closer he got to the counter, his face changed to one of sadness with tears in his eyes. 'My mother has died… what I am going to do?' I leaned over the bar to him and said, 'Bury her.' He was not amused and left the bar cursing me from a height.

One afternoon a while later, I was walking down Grafton Street when I heard the unmistakable sound of his voice. Coming face to face, we looked each other in the eye as we passed each other. I knew by his face that he was not too sure about who I was. When out of uniform, it is surprising how many people don't know me straightaway. From behind me, I heard his roar, 'You're that bastard from the Shelbourne Hotel.' Everyone looked around and I just kept on walking. I could still hear him roaring as I walked farther away. That was the last encounter that I had with him. I have seen him in many plays and a few films and he seems to have gotten his life together. I wonder if he ever buried his mother?

Scruffy Murphy

Paddy Mulligan was the sort of man you heard before you saw. He was the boss of Scruffy Murphy's and was a handsome, big man with a mass of white hair. He enjoyed being in the limelight, though he could be very difficult after a few drinks.

He headed a consortium from Scruffy Murphy's who won the lotto and did they have some party. From what you could see, most in the syndicate had a problem – the win didn't bring them any luck. With a few drinks, they were off the wall totally. One evening, I had the misfortune of having to bar him because of his behaviour, though he still appeared in the Horseshoe from time to time. One day, he approached the counter and I said, 'No, Paddy, you know the rules.'

He said, 'Please, Sean, there are some people that I have to meet here.'

The people that he was to meet were staying in the hotel and suggested meeting in the Horseshoe. He pleaded with me and explained that this was a very important meeting. I told him it was okay if he behaved. He told me that he was negotiating a contract for an Australian wine. He had assured the Australians that he could distribute the wine in all of the bars and restaurants in Ireland.

When the party arrived, he retreated to a corner table. There was a lot of toing and froing to the bar and Paddy got a bit tipsy and really messed up the meeting. The Australians got up and left the table and that seemed to be the end of that. He said they were to return later with their decision, needless to say, they never returned. Paddy was his own worst enemy. He was full of big ideas but none of them ever worked, as work got in the way. For all of that, he was not the worst. Whenever we meet in the street, he was always very courteous.

The Man from the *Irish Press*

Sean Kilfeather was one of those people who you knew was weighing you up from when you first met him. I don't know what happened between them but himself and Eamon Dunphy did not get on at all. Sean had a fabulous voice and if he hadn't got into journalism, he could have made his name as a singer.

He sat at the counter having his drink – he loved his pint of Guinness or glass of whiskey – discussing the sport of the day. Hs great passion was boxing and he loved talking about the great boxers of old. Without warning, he would suddenly break into song. I would say, 'No singing, Sean', and he would just ignore me. When he had finished, he always received a great round of applause, to which I would say, 'Don't encourage him.'

Other times, he arrived at the door, looked in and burst into song just to see what I would do. He arrived in one day and asked if he could sing and I said no. The only time we allow singing in the Horseshoe was on a rugby weekend. He would say to me, 'Come on, we're both northern men' – Sean was from Sligo. We had many a discussion about Northern politics and the GAA. The singing continued.

One day, I said, 'Sean, I'll make a deal with you, the day you come in and sing 'The Sash My Father Wore' in Irish (he was a fluent Irish speaker), I will let you sing.'

He said, 'You're on', and, at that, he left.

The Olympics were on and I had not seen him for some time. Out of the blue one evening at about 7 p.m., I head this singing and, looking around, saw Sean was standing in the doorway, singing his heart out. I recognised the tune but not the words and as he continued, you could hear a pin drop and the bar was fairly busy. When he finished, he received rousing applause and he came to the bar and asked, 'Now can I sing? That was 'The Sash' in Irish.'

I knew he had me, and the staff were waiting for my reaction. I was in serious trouble. I had visions of Sean arriving every day, singing his heart out.

I replied, 'Sean, how do I know that was 'The Sash'?'

He looked at me and said, 'You Northern bastard', and lucky for me he did not hold me to my bargain. Sean was a contrary, little man who could be very difficult at times, but was always interesting. Sadly, he is no longer with us.

The Man from the *Evening Press*

Con Houlihan's most famous column was on the back page of the *Evening Press* where he wrote as a sports correspondent. He was also, at one point, the education correspondent as he had previously been a secondary school teacher in County Kerry. He addressed me as 'my friend from Antrim' and we had many talks about the GAA in the North as he supped his favourite drink, a brandy and milk. When the *Irish Press* closed its doors, he was completely lost and drifted from paper to paper. I met him one evening and asked how he was. I wasn't certain who he was writing for. Holding his hand to his face, which he usually did, he said, 'Sean, I'm working for a comic.'

Kevin McClory

Kevin McClory was a wonderful character from County Down who stayed in the hotel quite a lot. He served in the merchant navy on the convoys in the North Atlantic during the Second World War. He claimed fame some years later as producer of some of the James Bond films. He also had some dispute about writing credits and was in the process of suing the film company – the suit went on for years. He would camp up in his room for weeks at a time working on a new James Bond script… or so he said.

He visited the Horseshoe from time to time. His drink was Jack Daniels and, by God, he could he drink it. One evening, he had a few friends in and asked to run a tab.

At the end of the night, he was standing in rather a peculiar position hanging over at a right angle. The bartender presented the bill, which was quite hefty, for payment. He took the bill and scrutinised it. It contained several Southern Comforts, which was the till key we used for Jack Daniels as it was the same price. Kevin tried to straighten himself and said, 'I am not paying for Southern Comforts, I did not have them.' We explained to him but he did not want to know and refused to pay for the drinks. He told the bartender that if they were not taken off of the bill, he would not pay for any of it, so I deducted the Southern Comforts and he paid the bill.

The following evening, he arrived in again. I asked him if he got back to his room okay and he replied, 'I must have. I can't remember much of last night.'

I said, 'You remember you left a small bill behind?' He apologised and said he would pay it straight away. He paid it and left a healthy tip. I think it was the only time I ever got at tip from him.

Kevin was working on a film in Ardmore Studios one day; he came back from the set on very bad form. Apparently, someone on the set, not knowing who he was, had told him to keep his grandson under control. He blew up and sacked the guy on the spot. The 'grandson' in question was his son, Sean, who was about six years of age and was starring in the film.

Another evening, Kevin arrived into the Horseshoe with Daragh O'Malley. Daragh, as I mentioned earlier, was a theatrical agent and was looking after Kevin's son. There was a problem over Sean's name as another actor was also called Sean McClory. Daragh said, 'We'll have to find a way around this.' At about 4 a.m. the following morning, Kevin phoned Daragh who was less than pleased. 'Daragh I have the answer. We will call him Sean 'T'. McClory'. That is how Sean got his stage name.

One evening, Dessie Hynes, who owned O'Donoghue's at the time, was in the Horseshoe and in Kevin's company. He mentioned that he needed a grand piano for a function that he was organising. Kevin said, 'I have one, you can use it whenever you like.' Dessie was delighted. The night wore on and Dessie asked where he could collect the piano. Kevin says, 'It's in the front room of my house in the Bahamas.'

Shane McGowan

Shane stayed in the Shelbourne a few times. He arrived into the bar one evening, much the worse for the wear. My daughter, Etain, was behind the counter and when she saw the state he was in, she took him to one side, got a tissue and cleaned the white powder from his face. She refused to serve him and guided him to the lift and back to his room.

Shane is a wonderful songwriter. 'The Fairytale of New York' is one of the finest Christmas songs ever written, expressing the cruelty of the world in which we live, and the sadness often felt at Christmas, but also shows the humour and happiness.

While I am writing about Shane, I want to mention a lady in the Horseshoe one evening who became quite difficult. I asked her to leave and she refused saying that her family use the hotel regularly and that her brother had stayed there. They often had afternoon tea in the Lords Mayor's Lounge. I asked her who her brother was, she said Shane McGowan!

Edna O'Brien

Edna usually stayed in the Shelbourne when she was in town. The first book I read of hers was *The Girl With Green Eyes* and it left quite an impression on me. I never thought that, one day, I would meet her and she would discuss a new book that she was researching with me as she sat casually sipping a drink in the Horseshoe. Edna is one of the stars of Irish fiction. Her beauty astounded people in the bar, even those who didn't know her for her literary fame. She was born Tuamgraney, County Clare, in 1930. In 1950, she was awarded a licence as a pharmacist and practised in Dublin. In 1954, she married, against her parents' wishes, the Czech–Irish writer Ernest Gebler – uncle of Stan Gebler

Davies, whom we meet elsewhere these pages – who died in 1998. Edna was hugely influenced by James Joyce and came to write extensively about him. She published her first book, *The Country Girls*, in 1960.

Liam Lawlor

Liam Lawlor, of tribunal fame, was not a regular but came in from time to time, usually on a Saturday night. He was a pleasant enough man, his drink was a gin and tonic.

He enjoyed people coming up to him to discuss the tribunal and enjoyed telling the stories of when he was in jail, why he was there and how the other prisoners treated him like a little tin god. How he loved to talk about those times and joke about the brown-paper envelopes. I always felt he was having the last laugh on those who hung on to his every word.

Noelle Campbell Sharp

I have known Noelle Campbell Sharp for many years. She used to frequent the old Hibernian Hotel in Dawson Street. In those days, she was working on her magazines and had a few to her name. She was a frequent visitor to the Horseshoe Bar and enjoyed her glass of champagne. She had an account with me, a privilege which few were given.

Noelle drove a beautiful, old Bentley and also had a custom-built sports car, which she loved. In the late 1980s, she started up the Cill Rialaig Artist Retreat charity project in Bulus Head, near Ballinscelligs, County Kerry. Noelle had discovered an abandoned famine village and transformed it into a cultural centre for visiting artists from around the world, who found inspiration and peace there. I also knew her partner, Niall McGuinness, brother to U2's Paul. Niall had invited me down for a fishing trip and was to finalise the details upon his next visit to Dublin. Unfortunately, he died of a heart attack a few days after inviting me.

CBS's *60 Minutes*

Mary Finnegan, correspondent and author, was Ireland's representative for CBS's *60 Minutes*. She was interviewing a gentleman from the west of Ireland about his life and was finding it very difficult to pin him down and get him to stick to the subject. I think he was more interested in Mary than he was in the interview. The camera crew were from the US and could not believe that this guy was for real. Eventually, the interview was over and everyone took a big sigh of relief. The man asked Mary when the programme would be shown and she said it would be in a week or two. He said that he was looking forward to seeing himself on television. He enquired of one of the crew if they had enough material to cover the sixty minutes. The crewman looked at him and said, 'You won't be on for sixty minutes, *60 Minutes* is the name of the programme.'

'What do you mean, I won't be on for sixty minutes. How long will I be on for?'

The guy answered, 'If you are lucky, you might get two or three minutes.'

The man from the west looked at him and asked what the interview was all about – the last I saw of him he was looking for Mary. Luckily for her, she had gone. When the programme was aired, he got a fair time of fifteen minutes of a very entertaining programme.

Virginia Cole – Part II

Actress and star of large and small screen Virginia drives a beautiful sports Mercedes. She would always fly up Kildare Street, turn right into the Shelbourne car park, stop outside the office, throw the keys to Charlie and say, 'I'm off to the Horseshoe.'

Charlie would roar after her, 'You can't park here.'

Virginia would answer, 'I'm off now… see you tomorrow.'

Virginia was a bit like Imelda Marcos and had shoes for all occasions – shoes to drive, shoes to walk and shoes to make her entrance to the Horseshoe. From time to time, I would remind her that we had several pairs of her shoes in the backroom and not to forget them.

Kevin Moore

Successful property developer, Kevin Moore was a regular in the Horseshoe from the early 1990s. His drink in those days was a pint of potato water, otherwise known as Smithwicks. He used to stand with his back to the large mirror watching the staff. George and I used to wonder who he was. Through time, we got to know him and found him to be a very nice man, a real Dub and a gent. He has helped out quite a few people. He also became a friend. Kevin has a very successful business. He is the boss of a bricklaying company which works on major Irish and international contracts.

He was a friend of David Duane. When I say friend, I mean good friend. Kevin was also a friend of Patrick Gallagher and invested money in a business that Patrick was running in South Africa, something to do with property. However, it did not go well and everyone lost out.

A Doctor in the House

Dr Flood lived in the Shelbourne for many years and was the unofficial doctor for the hotel, though her real practice is in Gardiner Street. Her constant companion was her little white poodle which she worshipped. Dr Flood drove a green Porsche, one of the few of its kind around in the 1980s and 1990s. It was stolen on numerous occasions but she always got it back.

One day, she was waiting for the lift to go to her room and was in conversation with another guest. When the lift arrived, they both entered. In the old lift, you had to pull the gate across before the lift started. Unfortunately, the poodle did not get on the lift and was outside, still on its leash. The lift started up and the dog was drawn towards the lift. Other guests in the Lobby looked on in amazement and could not believe the sight of the dog climbing up the gate of the lift. Luckily, the lift was only going to the first floor and the dog was left hanging when it stopped. Dr Flood was very relieved to see her dog arrive safely to the ground floor unscathed by its ordeal, as were the onlookers in the Lobby.

The Wedding

Ian McGlinchey, son of John, the man from Zimbabwe, and his beautiful partner of many years decided to get married and the ceremony was to take place in Dublin. The wedding party booked into the Shelbourne and, on the morning of the wedding, Ian was in the Horseshoe having a pre-wedding drink with some of his guests when he received a phone call to say that the Dubliner Pub in Gothenburg had been broken into. A JCB had been driven thorough the front of the bar, straight into the office and had lifted the safe. I heard him ask if any of the staff were hurt. He said not to worry as everything was insured. He turned to me and said, 'Let's get on with what we are here for.' The wedding reception was down in Dunbrody House in County Wexford, a place Ian used to own along with his business partner, Kevin Dundon, the celebrity chef.

Seventieth Birthday Party

Ian McGlinchey held a seventieth birthday party for his father in Gothenburg, Sweden. Ian lives there and has a very successful business – he owns the Dubliner bar and restaurant chain. He invited both myself and Josephine, my wife, to the party. Unfortunately, we arrived in Sweden before our luggage. The party was black tie and I looked particularly well in my runners and T-shirt, not to mention Josephine who was not at all amused. The party was at Ian's house, a fabulous place on the harbour in Gothenburg – he has a one-hole golf course in his front lawn. We spent three days there during the mid-summer festival and had a wonderful time.

Lillies Bordello

A few friends of Ian McGlinchey were staying in the Shebourne when they came to Ireland for a few days on a golfing trip. Ian asked me to organise a table for them in Lillies Bordello. I rang Valerie Roe, who was the manager, and asked her if she could organise this for me. She said she was not sure but she would check with the bouncers and get back to me. I could not believe what I was hearing and asked her who was running Lillies – her or the bouncers? They got in with no problem and had a great night. Ian said a wonderful lady called Jean Crowley looked after them very well.

The Man with the Ponytail

David Duane and his beautiful partner, Amber, arrived in Dublin from Adare Manor in County Limerick some time in 1995. He was larger than life and was known as a great character who had reinvented the hamburger. He was one of the great American meat barons. He sold his company in the US for several million and bought it back again for a few dollars, or so the story goes. David and Amber were a stylish couple about town and had a box at the RDS for the

Horseshow, money was no object. They resided in the Shelbourne for months at a time and, the longer they stayed, the more friends they made. Of course, this kind of life also attracts chancers but he was wise to these guys. He was a good friend of Dave and Mairead Egan of Lillies Bordello and Bruxelles of Harry Street.

David decided to settle down in Ireland. Amber was involved in horses, so they looked for a place around Naas, County Kildare. They asked a regular of ours, Oliver Caffrey, if he could find an estate for them and Oliver found them a place just outside of Kill. They bought it, renamed it Amberleigh Lodge and carried out extensive renovations – and also built an indoor equestrian centre. His parties during the Punchestown spring festival were legendary. They went on all night and, the next day, everyone went on from Amberleigh Lodge to the races. When the racing was over, the partying started all over again. David had several race horses, one called Amberleigh House with which he had great success. In latter years, it won the Aintree Grand National, although he was not its owner at that time.

David and Amber were the real couple about town, throwing lavish parties in Lillies Bordello. David's drink was Bud Light but when it was withdrawn from the market, he moved on to Coors Light.

Unfortunately, parties do not last forever. In later years, the couple split and Amber and went to live in Argentina. It seemed as though she had taken the fun-loving side of David with her as, sadly, all that remained was a lonely, old man. David missed Amber terribly and though he went out with a few of the so-called starlets of the day, the relationships never lasted. He sold Amberleigh Lodge and moved into town. He leased the famous penthouse in Huguenot House and spent his mornings sitting over a Coors Light in the Horseshoe. James Craig would be sitting on one side of the bar and David on the other, the only thing passing between them was a bit of small talk.

David was invited to Michael Flatley's Christmas party in London, when *Lord of the Dance* was running there. Dave and Mairead Egan were also invited and went over with him. After the party, David returned to his hotel and suffered a stroke in his sleep and was in hospital for several weeks. Eventually, when he arrived back in Dublin, he was in a wheelchair. It was sad to see someone who had not so long ago been the cock of the walk this way. He was also still in Huguenot House and was still coming in to the Horseshoe with his minder, but he was not the same. Sometime later, he had a very serious fire in the penthouse; it was so serious that the Shelbourne had to be evacuated. The Conrad Hotel opened its doors to the residents; it was only what you would expect from a good hotel. David was accommodated at the Westbury and later moved to 8 Merrion Street. By this time, he had left the chair behind and was using a stick. He still came into the Horseshoe for his daily Coors Light. Then, one Wednesday, he failed to appear and was never seen again. I heard afterwards that he had returned to LA. He was also a good friend of Kevin Moore's and would have dinner at his place once a week.

Vi Lawlor

Vi Lawlor is a wonderful lady and one of the finest to ever grace the Horseshoe. She was a legend in Ireland's bloodstock industry. I can still hear her, 'Sean, a glass of shampoo.' She was always up to devilment.

I first met her when Forte owned the Shelbourne and, every year, we had a race day in the Phoenix Park. On one particular day, I had the good fortune of being her escort. She asked me what I knew about racing, to my shame I admitted that it was not one of my vices at which she laughed. 'I will teach you. Come along', so off we went. She introduced me to the parade ring. I said I knew nothing about horses and asked what I should be looking for. She threw me a look and told me that we were not there for the horses; it was the trainers and the owners we wanted – and did she know them all! On the first and second races, we backed the winner. I was getting very excited at this stage and wanted to know what the next race was. Her reply was, 'Enough racing for now… we will go for afternoon tea. Come along.'

I asked, 'Aren't we going to back anymore?'

She replied, 'Not for the moment.'

The fifth race was coming up and she said, 'I think we will go and have another bet', and, would you believe it, we won again! She then said, 'It's back to the Forte tent for a glass or two of shampoo.' What a fabulous lady, one of the true racing greats.

Arthur McCoy

A gentleman with an eastern European accent asked if I knew Arthur McCoy, and, if so, would it be possible for me to get a phone number for him. Arthur was one of Ireland's early beef barons. I told the man that if he left me his number, I would arrange a meeting. A meeting was then set up for them in the Horseshoe Bar. This chap wanted Arthur to arrange for a consignment of intervention beef to be exported to some part of Russia. The only problem with this was that the potential customers had no money. What they did have was several dozen diesel motor boat engines that had been ordered by the Russian government but, because of the economic crisis in the mid-1980s, the order had been cancelled. He and Arthur hammered out some deal using the barter system, I was unsure of the details. I never did find out the outcome but such deals were common place in the Horseshoe Bar in the recession-ridden 1980s.

Arthur the Traveller

Arthur McCoy travelled all over the world at one time or another – Australia, South America, the USA, South Africa, Cuba, and many other places were all just another local journey for him.

He told me a great story of something that happened during his time in Australia. He was sitting in the Horseshoe Bar one day having a drink prior to his departure for Australia when he got into a conversation with one of the duty managers. Arthur happened to mention that he was off to Australia and the manager told him that he had a brother out there and named the place where he was living. When Arthur was in Australia, he was travelling from one place to another by bus and he saw a place name which he thought was familiar. When he returned to his hotel room that evening, he called the Shelbourne to find out if this was the place where the manager's brother lived. It turned out that it was and the manager gave Arthur his brother's phone number. Arthur rang the number and arranged for a meeting. The chap told him that he was away but would return within the week. He arranged to meet him in a bar in that town the following Friday. When the day arrived, Arthur arranged for the hotel to book him a taxi to take him to the bar. The hotel was not happy about Arthur going to this place but would not say why. The taxi driver wasn't happy about it either, but Arthur, being Arthur, was now more determined to go than ever.

When he arrived at the bar, he was amazed to see that it was nothing more than a shack in the middle of the bush with no civilisation visible for miles. The taxi driver told Arthur that he would wait for him as he would need to get back and no other taxi drivers would come out that far. As Arthur walked to the front door of the bar, he wondered what he was going to meet. He walked in and there was a pool table, a couple of pinball machines and about a dozen people, including the bartender. As he said, it took him a few minutes to adjust to the darkness after all that time out in the sun. As he walked up to the bar, he said that he felt like someone out of the nineteenth century in a saloon in the wild west. All heads were turned towards him. When he asked the bartender if the fellow he was looking for was there, they all sat up and a great silence fell over the room. Arthur wondered what he had said that was wrong.

The barman looked at Arthur and asked him if he was a friend of this man. Arthur replied that he wasn't, that he was just there to meet him. The barmen told him that the man was not there. Arthur ordered a beer and settled down to wait. Eventually, a rather large man entered the bar and, again, silence fell on the bar. The man walked straight up to Arthur and asked, 'Are you McCoy?' Arthur said he was and ordered another drink. The bartender told him that he would serve him but his companion was not welcome in the bar.

Arthur had sensed the animosity before he had even ordered the man a drink. He ordered two beers to go and they left the bar. They spent some time talking outside before Arthur returned to his hotel. On the way back in the taxi, the driver explained to Arthur that the bar had been the main outlet for range drovers. These guys would travel hundreds of miles a day with cattle and sheep. They were lacking greatly in manners and etiquette. The man Arthur had met was the manager of a sheep station about 200 miles away and was one of the hardest and least-liked men in those parts. When Arthur retuned to his room, he thought about his afternoon and said to himself, 'There's a black sheep in every family.' He sent a card the following day to tell me of his adventures.

Michael Collins

The filming of the movie *Michael Collins* was a very exciting time for the Shelbourne. It was in the mid-1990s. All the big stars sayed in the hotel – Julia Roberts, Liam

George Duffy with Sean behind the bar, dressed for action.

George Duffy making his award-winning cocktail, Salsa.

This is a photograph of many faces — how many do you recognise?

Des Benson and James Craig. Two long-standing regulars – putting the world to rights.

The dapper John McGlinchey with his wife Claire.

P.J. Mara, former
press secretary to
Charles Haughey.

CEO of Riverdeep
and former
bartender at the
Shelbourne, Barry
O'Callaghan.

Sean, Cyril Kelly and Mike Burns.

Senior counsel Gerry Danaher, holding court in the Shelbourne.

Scan with John Cooney, the director of the Humbert Summer School, and Bertie Ahern.

Scan with Nobel prize winner John Hume

Dr John Wallace
having the 'auld craic'
in the Horseshoe.

Oliver Bardon, of
O'Donoghue's, and
beef baron Jim
Gleeson enjoying a
quiet drink.

Neeson, Alan Rickman and Aidan Quinn. There was a real buzz about the place. Every evening, Julia Roberts would return from filming and come straight in to me in the bar and ask that I look after her entourage of about forty people. She made sure they were okay before she even thought about going to her room. This was my assignment every day. I went to Timmy Spilane in Banquets on the first floor to make sure everything was set up.

One evening, I was talking with the director, Neil Jordan, and asked him who was playing the part of Joe Dolan. He looked at me in amazement and asked how I knew this person. I told him that I had met Joe in 1959 in my uncle's pub the Harbour Lights Bar in Echlin Street. Neil asked me a few things about Joe. I told him the story of the shooting of Sergeant Roche in Amiens Street. I also told him that Joe wrote a book entitled *I Carried a Gun for Michael Collins* but, unfortunately, it was never published. The government of the time were in great opposition to the book as there were a lot of people still alive who would be affected by its content.

For those unfamiliar with Joe Dolan, he was a member of Michael Collins' elite. He was his most trusted confidante and right-hand man. When the negotiations for the Treaty were going on in 1921, King George V asked to meet Joe as he had great admiration for him and his exploits. Sadly, Joe is not remembered today as he should be.

Scrap Saturday

Dermot Morgan dropped into the bar occasionally to say hello. Ironically, he always insisted on a priest's head of over an inch long on his pint of Guinness. During his series of *Scrap Saturday*, Dermot referred to P.J. Mara being in the Horseshoe Bar doing business for 'the boss'. The management of the hotel at that time were far from amused at this and wrote to him about it. They did not like the Horseshoe being referred to as the 'Horseshit Bar'. Dermot wrote back saying, 'I called it the Horse*shite* Bar.' A management meeting was called to discuss this and to propose that Mr Morgan be barred from the hotel. This was met with great opposition and so the proposal was dropped. Little did management realise that it was people like Mara who made the place popular with the general public.

John Hume

John Hume was regular in the Horseshoe whenever he was in town. One morning, he was sitting in the bar reading the *Independent* and discovered that Eamon Dunphy had written an article about him being in league with the IRA. John was very distressed by this allegation. Shortly afterwards, Eamon sauntered into the bar and ordered a bottle of Becks. John Hume challenged him over the article, shouting, 'That article you wrote could have me shot.' A row ensued between the two and, at one stage, it got very heated, so much so that I had to ask Eamon to leave the bar. The management heard of this and ordered that Dunphy be barred. John was extremely upset and it took quite a while to console him. Later that day, John returned to the bar and apologised to both the management and myself for what had occurred, saying that he did not wish to see Eamon Dunphy barred.

Dunphy

Eamon Dunphy, was another bane of my life. I never knew what to expect when I saw him coming. He sometimes stood at the bar and shout across it in my direction, 'There's Sean the Provo from the Falls Road.' People would look around, wondering who he was referring to. I often thought I would end up shot myself. On nights like this, I would hope that Eamon's tipple was a bottle of Becks and not a champagne cocktail as he was easier to handle when he had the beer.

He is immensely popular with a lot of people and hated by others. I was aware of the fact that people used to come to the bar just to look at him. He once said that this phenomenon gave him a perfect understanding of how the animals in the zoo felt.

The BBC

In 1996, the BBC had a programme on Radio 4 called *Am I Still Standing?* The programme visited ten cities throughout the world searching for the ten best bars. At this stage, they had visited the 21 Club in New York, Harry's Bar in Venice and then it was our turn in the Horseshoe Bar. The programme covered the drinks, staff and, of course, the celebrities that frequented the ten bars. The Horseshoe was also voted by *Time* magazine as one of the top bars of the world.

Our Own Lord Nelson

Mr Nelson was a very mysterious character who only ever appeared at night. We know that he used to live with us for a many years despite owning properties in Bombay, London, Paris and New York. He was always dressed in a tweed jacket and black trousers – I had visions of rows upon rows of these jackets hanging in his room – which made some people think he was a bit peculiar. He is a lovely man with a very gentle nature. He liked to stand outside the Horseshoe Bar and order a glass of red wine – he enjoyed being on his own and spoke to very few people, but he always had a smile and a nod for everyone.

Early one morning, he arrived back to the hotel. The night manager, who was new, was not familiar with Mr Nelson and refused to let him in, so he stood at the door for the whole night until the morning staff came on. They were very upset that he had not been allowed in. He was the sort of character who would order a taxi to take him to Temple Bar and would go from bar to bar until closing time. Then, he would arrive back to the hotel and spend the night chatting to the night staff about the ways of the world.

It was said that someone told him a story of a hill some place in Ireland where water appeared to flow up instead of down. He was intrigued by this story and often brought it up in conversation. Eventually, he found out the name of the place, got into a taxi and drove straight there. I think the taxi man thought he was mad. When they arrived at the designated place, he got out of the taxi, went to the back of it and peed down the hill to see if it would run back up. Whether or not it did, I will never know. When he was finished, he got back into the taxi and said, 'Take me back to the Shelbourne.'

Mrs Keane

Love her or hate her, Terry Keane was a legend. She achieved fame in Ireland for two things – as a gossip columnist for the *Sunday Independent* and as the mistress of Charlie Haughey. Indeed, the two things quite often went hand in hand. Born in England, she came to Trinity College Dublin to study medicine but abandoned those studies to become a journalist. Her wit was legendary. Her capacity for the putdown was infinite. Once, in the Horseshoe Bar, she was overheard complaining about the standard of public transport in Ireland. Someone shouted over to her, 'For Jaysus sake, Terry, when were you ever on a bus?' To which she replied, 'My dear, I'm not talking about the buses, I'm talking about Aer Lingus!'

I only saw her in the Horseshoe with Charlie Haughey once. Their affair was conducted mostly in Le Coq Hardi, a restaurant in nearby Pembroke Road. She wrote a great deal about the goings on in the Horseshoe Bar throughout the 1980s and 1990s. Hardly a week went by when she did not have a story from the bar. She had extraordinary presence. When she was in the bar there was a sense of frisson and people were always looking at the corner she was sitting in. She was eventually cornered by some 'friends' in *The Sunday Times* to sell the story of her love affair. It was published to shock-horror gasps around the country and did her enormous damage. She was very badly advised under pressure and, in a way, the whole thing destroyed her health. She did not live to see the old age that she should have enjoyed, but her memory will live on as one of the great characters produced by Ireland.

P.J. Mara's Brunch

In 1992, when P.J. was leaving office as Charlie Haughey's press secretary, a brunch was organised in his honour by Paul McGuinness and Eamon Dunphy. The brunch was held in Room 112, the Constitution Room. I was asked to be in attendance after the meal when everything had been cleared away,. They wanted no other staff in the room – only me. The guests sat down to brunch at about 4 p.m. and didn't leave the room until 7 a.m. the following morning. Twenty-nine people sat at the table with only three ladies amongst them. Rhona Tiernan, Rhona Blake and Mary Holland. When the table had been cleared and all staff had left the room, I was left to attend to the big, oval table. There was a very informal atmosphere with people conversing at will, each with their own story to tell. Paul McGuinness told a story of P.J. saying to him, 'What you have done for U2, I have done for C.J.' Paul reminded him that he got 20 per cent of U2 but asked did he get 20 per cent of C.J.? Dermot Desmond spoke of loyalty and qualities that P.J. had and reminded those at the table that, despite their success, they had come from humble beginnings.

Sam Smyth was introduced as the man who exposed the Greencore scandal. Someone interrupted the introduction and stated that those people were all crooks who had stolen the Irish people's money. He said that he would not have missed the evening for the world as they had been through both good and bad together and, just like P.J., he too had lost his job. There was a rapturous applause for this. Mary Holland spoke of her days in *The Observer* and how she was sacked over political wrangling and that P.J. was a great friend who had helped her through those bad days. Eamon Dunphy was introduced by Ray Burke as an upstart of a journalist also known as a Mickey Mouse footballer.

The speeches continued on late into the night and into the morning. At the end of a function, it is customary for the person in charge of the room, in this case me, to have the bill signed or collect a cheque. Paul McGuinness and Eamon Dunphy could not agree on who would foot the bill, so I suggested that we would leave it as it was and sort it out later. To this day, I do not know if that was ever paid. The press were all over the place trying to find out who was there and what was said. Many incentives were offered to me but not a word was spoken. the *Irish Times* supplement that weekend was the only paper to get the details of the story right. The *Independent* got it all wrong – the details of Ray Burke's outburst were completely inaccurate. He did not say he'd rather resign than be sacked.

The Pheasant, the Fish and the Green-Haired Painter

Mick Mulcahy, well what can I say about this extraordinary man? In the 1990s, when I first met Mick, I had a full head of hair, now I am in my sixties and am bald. He was a wild-looking character with a distant look in his eyes but he possessed a great charm and character in such abundance that I was very cautious of him. One of his favourite drinks, when he was drinking, was Pernod Coffee, a crazy combination by any standards. Over the years that I knew this man, I think I barred him from the Horseshoe about twenty times, but he still kept coming in. He always appealed to my better nature to give him another chance, sometimes arms stretched out pleading, and I invariably give in.

One afternoon, he was drinking in the bar with several of his friends. They had been there for a few hours. At one stage, he approached the bar and, in a sheepish voice, asked if he could have credit, to which I answered no. He apologised for asking and left the bar. A few moments later, he returned with two sheets of paper which I presume he had got from Reception. He took a bar stool, sat up on it and started to sketch the party he was with. When he had finished he said to me, 'Don't throw these fellows out, I will be back shortly.' He arrived back about half an hour later with a beaming smile gave the boys a drink and handed me a cheque for £250 from the National Gallery in Merrion Square. What I failed to mention in my opening was that Mick Mulcahy is a very accomplished artist with a huge critical reputation worldwide. Over the years, Mick wandered in and out of the bar, we had our differences but w never fell out.

He came in one day and told me that he had just received a commission for several large paintings for the Chinese embassy and that he was going off to Connemara to do the work. After that, I didn't seen Mick for quite a while until, one day, he arrived in and in all his majesty announced that he was going off to North Korea to a Buddhist temple to find himself. I wished him all the best of luck and set him up a drink for the road.

Four years passed and no sign of Mick. He entered my mind from time to time as Dublin was very dull without him. One Saturday morning, I heard his voice and knew he was back. He stood at the door of the Horseshoe larger than life, his hair was dyed green and the crown of his head was shaved in the shape of a bird's nest. He was wearing a leopard-skin cloak with a large, brown belt around his waist which held two Samurai swords, one large one small. His arms were laden down with flowers. I stood and wondered at this creature at the door. He roared at me, 'Sean, it's good to be home.' He proceeded over to the bar laying out his flowers along the bar counter. He took out a porcelain figure from the bag he had on his shoulder. It was of an old man squatting and he placed it in the centre of the flowers. I stared gobsmacked in wonder and amazement. He then proceeded to take out a small mat which I presumed was a prayer mat. He was about to get down on his knees when I intervened and told him the bar was not a church or a monastery. He jumped up grabbing the mat and ran out the door shouting at the top of his voice. What he said I don't know. I cleared the figurine and the flowers from the counter. I still have the very same figurine to this day. A few hours later, the gardaí came into the bar and asked if I had seen a fellow with green hair and a leopard-skin cloak with two swords. I told them that I knew the person they were talking about. They told me that he had been in Grafton Street squatting in the middle of street and when they approached him he ran off shouting, 'I am going back to the Shelbourne.' Later, he arrived back in and the gardaí quickly took the swords from him.

Not long after this incident, Mick returned to Galway. I read in the papers that he had got married under the Brehon Laws – an old Gaelic ceremony which took place on a boat. Needless to say, he was divorced in a similar manner not too long afterwards.

It was many years before I met Mick again. He arrived into the bar full of life carrying a box tied with twine. He told me that he was on the wagon and asked me to take care of the box, saying that he would return later that evening for it. I forgot all about it and, some days later, I noticed a very strange odour from the back of the bar. I asked my staff where it was coming from. Eventually, George Duffy discovered that the smell was coming from the box Mick had left. Opening the box, I discovered two dead pheasants, one hen and one cock. I hadn't a clue what to do with them, so I spoke with the chef in the kitchen who offered to put them in the cooling fridge. This took place on a Thursday… by Saturday, Mick still hadn't collected them so I went back to the chef and said that I would give a demonstration on how to pluck and cook a pheasant to his commis chefs. He agreed. I had a full attendance of commis chefs that evening for the demonostration. I had been told that the birds would not last much longer, so I took them home and ate them for Sunday lunch.

Several weeks later, Mick arrived in and announced that he had fallen off the wagon! I asked him if he was in to collect his pheasants. He looked at me in amazement and said, 'This is where I left the f'in things. What did you do with them?' I told him I had them for lunch, to which he replied, 'You were just right.'

He then proceeded to go into the whole saga of how he had got them and who they were for. Of course, he could not remember what he had done with them. He then asked me if I like salmon to which I replied, 'Of course I like salmon.'

A few days later, one of the concierges came into the bar and told me that a parcel had arrived for me by courier. When I opened it, there was a full fresh salmon and a note from Mick simply saying, 'Enjoy.' After this incident, Mick seemed to fall off the face of the earth. I did not see him for a good many years. The last encounter I had with him was when he was holding an exhibition in Noelle Campbell Sharp's Urban Gallery in Grand Canal Dock. The paintings were all nudes… of himself!

The Scandal of Woody Allen and his Daughter

One summer afternoon, two American ladies were sitting at the bar enjoying a chat while their husbands were out playing golf. One of the ladies was looking out the door and noticed Woody Allen and Soon-Yi Previn, the adopted daughter of his former partner Mia Farrow, walking towards the lift.

She looked at her friend and said, 'That's Woody Allen.'

She asked me if they were staying in the hotel to which I replied, 'I don't know.'

The lady gave a knowing smile to her friend, advised that she was leaving the bar but would be back shortly. She returned a half an hour later and left a package with the porter to be delivered to Woody Allen's room.

A short time later, I noticed a commotion coming from the Lobby. A very enraged Mr Allen was demanding to know who had sent the package to his room. I went out to the lobby to see what was going on and saw Woody Allen holding up a T-shirt with 'I Love My Daddy' written across the front. Needless to say, he was far from amused. I then realised where the lady had disappeared to. She had gone to St Stephen's Green and had the T-shirt printed. The two ladies just sat there and smiled.

Six Cocktails for the Speakeasy Lady

Sissy Welch was in her eighties and on her third world cruise. She had read about the Horseshoe in a magazine on the ship and had flown to Dublin on a whim to stay in the hotel and have a drink in the bar. Every evening, she arrived down at 6 p.m., sat up at the bar and had her gin martini straight up. She used to say there was only on other person who could make a better martini than us and that was herself, and then she would laugh.

She told me about her life and I asked her if would she like to start life over again to which she replied, 'Definitely not.' She told me that in her youth, she did everything that was unacceptable. She drank, she smoked and she ran with the bad boys. She said that if she was starting out again today, there were so many drugs about that she reckoned she would not last too long. She said that, in her day, people looked after each other.

She had been in college during Prohibition and had found it difficult to fund her education, so she decided to set up her own speakeasy. This became a huge success and was frequented by both students and lecturers. It was an open secret which lasted right up to the end of Prohibition. The success of the speakeasy inspired her to drop out of college and open her own nightclub. Her business grew to include several bars and clubs over the 1930s, 1940s and 1950s. She ran them with the help of her husband, Jack. Sadly, Jack died in the early 1960s and she lost the passion for running her businesses. She sold up and went into retirement. With no family, she was left to face retirement alone but, not one to wallow in self-pity, she decided to travel the world. I asked her why she loved sitting at the bar and she told me it reminded her of the guys sitting at her bar. The concept of the bar had been the making of her vast fortune and she remained loyal to it.

The Birthday Present

An old lady in New York was asked what she would like for her eightieth birthday. She replied, 'I would like a weekend in Dublin's Shelbourne Hotel.' On her arrival, she went straight to the bar accompanied by her granddaughter. Unfortunately, it was a Friday evening which meant mayhem. We couldn't get her a seat, so I took her into Elizabeth in the Lord Mayor's Lounge and asked that she be well looked after.

I went in to check on her on my break and decided to sit with her and have a quick chat. She told me that when she was twelve years old, she had been sitting in a dentist's waiting room and had picked up a magazine. There was an article in it all about the Shelbourne in Dublin. She had been fascinated by this magical place and wanted to find out all she could about it. She established a network of friends from Ireland who would regularly send her articles about the hotel and, over the years, had built a large dossier of information and history of the

Shelbourne. Never did she dream that, one day, she would get to sleep in one of the rooms and have a drink in its famous bar.

I was amazed by her story which I immediately told to our manager, Jean Ricoux. He looked after the lady very well. I invited her to come to bar on a Saturday afternoon when things were a little more civilised. We opened a bottle of Veuve Clicquot to toast her birthday. She stayed with us for the weekend and finished her holiday with a tour of Ireland. She returned to America with her childhood dream realised. After her return home, she wrote a letter to the hotel thanking us for the wonderful welcome she had received and the exceptional service that she received throughout her stay.

John and Claire McGlinchey

John McGlinchey, with his wife, Claire, left Ireland many years ago to seek their fortune in Rhodesia, as it was then known. What can we say about this extraordinary man? He is larger than life, a wonderful storyteller, magnificent pianist, and enjoys a good pint of Guinness and all the finer things in life. Always the life and soul of the party, he played the piano in the Lounge until the small hours of the morning, keeping many a spellbound patron entertained.

Early one Saturday morning, he was seen heading for the not-yet-open Horseshoe Bar when the porter asked him where he was going. 'To the bar,' he said. The porter told him that there was no one in the bar. 'The man I'm looking for is in the bar,' he replied.

'Who would that be?' asked the porter.

'Arthur Guinness,' replied John.

John and Claire came to Ireland two or three times a year and always stayed with us at the Shelbourne. They always made a beeline for the Horseshoe Bar on their arrival. John walked around the bar looking at the bar stools until he found the one he was looking for (there were twelve bar stools but one of a different colour to the rest). He would then ask the person sitting on it could he have 'his' stool. He explained to the person that the was 'his' stool as it was the one his wife had been sitting on when he had proposed to her. Needless to say, no one ever refused when they had heard his story. When he had 'his' stool, John would prop his wife up on it and would have an evening discussing the woes present-day Zimbabwe.

Once, during a tiff with his wife, who had locked herself in their room, he bombarded the room with red roses, on the hour, every hour, until there were so many flowers, it was impossible to move in the room and they were spilling out on to the hall. Claire finally relented and there was a glorious reconciliation in the Horseshoe. Champagne all round.

The Dark Mr Hamilton

Mr Hamilton, a very strange man, stayed in the Shelbourne for a few weeks with his wife, child and two minders. He arrived into the bar each day and ordered a bottle of Bollinger at £85 a pop – a lot of money in 1998. He would then wander between the Lounge, the Lobby and the Bar all afternoon. Often, when he saw other people sitting in the Lounge, he would ask one of the servers to leave a bottle of Bollinger with them at his expense regardless of whether or not they wanted it. He came into the bar one day and asked Charlie Brady for a good brandy. When he had received it, he asked if it was the best that money can buy. Charlie told him that he had Louis XIII which was very expensive. Mr Hamilton asked for that too. When Charlie had handed over the brandy, he was told to leave the bottle. It appears that Mr Hamilton had acquired quite a taste for the expensive cognac as he drank quite a few bottles of it over the next few weeks. He would order a bottle of Bollinger on a daily basis in the Horseshoe, the Lounge and in the Shelbourne Bar. He would drink one glass from each bottle before moving on to the next one. The only company he was seen to keep was that of his two minders.

Early one morning, he arrived down with his child and the two minders. We never saw his wife as she never left their room. He ordered his usual bottle of Bollinger and I asked him what his plans were for the day. He told me they were going to feed the ducks in St Stephen's Green. I asked him what he planned to feed them with. He looked at me with a blank stare. I asked him to wait a minute. I went to the kitchen, put some breadcrumbs in a bag and gave them to his child. They all left the bar and went off to feed the ducks, himself, the minders and the child. No sooner had they left than they returned and one of the minders was told to take the child up to the room. Mr Hamilton left the bar to go into the Lounge and I asked the other minder why they had come back so soon. He told me that the had gone straight to the park and when they reached the duck pond Mr Hamilton had said to the child, 'There are the ducks', and emptied the whole bag of bread into the water. No sooner had he done this, than he turned to the child told her she had fed the ducks and it was time to go.

Many a bemused customer asked me who this guy was, but I didn't know. However, there is always someone who knows something and I received a letter from Arthur McCoy some weeks later with a newspaper cutting telling Mr Hamilton's story. He was from a distinguished family but had a rather, shall we say, colourful life in London, which might not always have lived up to the standards required for membership of a gentleman's club.

The Late, Great Jonathan Philbin Bowman

There was a sketch on Eamon Dunphy's Today FM show, which aired weeknights between 5 p.m. and 7 p.m., which was set in the Horseshoe Bar. The brunt of the humour was a long-suffering George, Princess Di and Jonathan Philbin Bowman.

Jonathan was a character and a half. He had a caustic wit – I often pitied for those on the receiving end of his sharp tongue – and made quite a reputation for himself at an early age as a writer and broadcaster. He was one of the most promising talents in Ireland but his life was tragically cut short in a freak accident. Further proof that those whom the gods love die young. The son of John Bowman, the famous broadcaster, Jonathan decided at an early age to make his own way in life. Partly, this involved having a child at a very young age. The boy, Saul, named after Saul Bellow, was practically raised in the Horseshoe Bar. Jonathan often wheeled in the pram with great fatherly pride.

I first came across Jonathan during my time in Banqueting. I worked on the first floor where all the windows overlook Stephen's Green and would see this young fellow cycling around the Green. I found him very striking as he had long, blond hair and wore sandals without socks in both winter and summer. In the latter years, his son, Saul, was carried on the back of his bike, but he still had those hallmark sandals and no socks. I only realised who he was when I saw him on television one evening – after which I often watched him on his quiz show.

It wasn't until I graduated to the dizzy heights of the Horseshoe Bar that I really got to know Jonathan and we became good friends. The thing about him was that he always had an opinion and could drink too much on occasion. He enjoyed having stand-up arguments with 'Navan Man' and the drunken politician, which I observed closely. He became very passionate about his opinions, especially with a few drinks on him, and would often need to be taken aside and told to calm down. Charlie and George could never understand how I tolerated him, but I always found him easy to handle.

On one occasion, he came to the bar very drunk and I refused to serve him. To my surprise, he became quite nasty, a side of him I had never seen before. With great difficulty, I eventually persuaded him to leave the bar. I offered to get him a taxi home but he refused. I walked him to the front door of the hotel and asked Jimmy, the concierge, to keep an eye on him. Jimmy later told me that he had left with some friends. Later that night, I received a call from Damien in Banqueting to tell me that Jonathan was the bar and was very drunk.

He asked me to come over as he didn't know what to do with him. When I arrived, I found Jonathan in a very bad way, so, once again, I tried to get him a taxi home when, suddenly, he seemed to take some type of seizure. Unsure of what was wrong, we called an ambulance which promptly arrived. The paramedics were very good, they calmed him down and got him into the ambulance, accompanied by his friend, and took him to a hospital – which one, I don't know. It was several weeks before he reappeared in the Horseshoe Bar. I went straight over to him put my arm around his shoulder, turned him around and walked him out the door. I explained to him that after the previous incident, there was no way I could serve him, nor could he be served in any area of the hotel ever again. He apologised profusely for his behaviour. I often came across him in the street afterwards and we were always very cordial to each other often stopping for the odd chat.

A few years later, Jonathan walked into the Horseshoe Bar and told me that he needed a big favour. He said that some people were in the Lounge and that he had to interview them. He asked if it were possible to do this and promised that he was not drinking. He told me that it would cause him great embarrassment if I were to refuse him. Of course I let him stay. When he had finished the interview, he came back into the bar to thank me and I thought to myself that enough time had passed and decided to let bygones be bygones. I said, 'Jonathan, you are welcome back to the Shelbourne, I know that what occurred that night will never occur again,' He assured me it would not.

He was a breath of fresh air to the place, someone who had a great rapport with all the customers and it was nice to see him back. He was in with me the day before he died and he seemed to be in good form. It was with great sadness that both Charlie and I learned of his death, when we were in the bar. We kept getting bulletins all through the evening and it felt as if a star had died. It would be wonderful to hear his take on the current recession and general goings on of the world of 2009.

Francis and Ian Stuart

Francis Stuart was a distinguished novelist. His mother was Iseult Stuart, the daughter of W.B. Yeats' muse, Maud Gonne MacBride. He was tall and angular, with a mop of snow-white hair. He drank vats of what he called 'old English'. This was a particularly sweet sherry of which he was very fond. He attracted a great deal of attention as much for his notoriety as his fame. He was accused of being a Nazi sympathiser because he made broadcasts from Berlin during the Second World War. His most famous novel is *Blacklist Section H* but he was also a fine poet. He was a friend of Ulick O'Connor who sometimes came to the bar with him.

His son, Ian, is a well-known sculptor who was married to the sculptor Imogen Stuart. Ian used come to the bar with his very pretty daughters and enjoyed a glass of champagne and catching up with old friends like Gareth Browne or some of his Wicklow neighbours. He enjoyed a great lunch in the Saddle Room in the days when it was Dublin's top meeting place and a great floor show was guaranteed.

Reggie Hastings

I first knew Reggie in the Royal Hibernian but he migrated to the Horseshoe when the Buttery closed. He is from the old class of Dublin merchant princes whose family lived on Elgin Road. His grandfather founded a major firm of veterinary pharmaceutical manufacturers and his father was a much decorated army officer.

Reggie was one of the greatest supporters of the Horseshoe, often spending long afternoons with Gareth Browne discussing art and life. He had a great interest in the architecture of the bar and a great passion for collecting architectural salvage and items of historical association with hotels. He moved to Spain for many years but always returned, like the swallows, to the Horseshoe whenever he was in town. He married the writer Kate Braithwaite, daughter of the former British ambassador to Moscow, Sir Roderick Braithwaite. Kate worked for, amongst others, *The Spectator* in London and various financial publications in London and Moscow.

The Builders

Much has been written in recent times about the Horseshoe Bar as the unofficial birthplace of the Celtic Tiger. There is more than a grain of truth in this and it would not be an exaggeration to claim that many of the big property deals which led to the creation of Ireland's boom were born in the bar. Friday nights saw many of the country's top property developers come in for a drink. It was a sort of unofficial exchange for these boys as they drifted in after lunch at the Unicorn and then moved seamlessly between the Horseshoe and Doheny & Nesbitts. The gossip writers were often seen circling this wagon train of developers along with a bevy of flusies looking for husbands or just a night on free champagne.

Father Confessor to the Horseshoe Bar

The Horseshoe was unique in many ways but none more so in that it had its own priest. This role fell to Fr Sean Quigley our most regular 'man of the cloth', who was known to all as 'Q'. He was patrician in manner and discoursed in at least half a dozen tongues to a wide circle of admirers. He had been born in Austria and was very much a cut above your average curate.

He wore a high Roman collar and a heather-coloured tweed jacket and walked with the aid of a malacca cane that had a rabbit's head in ivory which he referred to as 'Harry'. He was known as the 'priest to the gentry' and officiated at all the grand baptisms, weddings and funerals, including the wedding of another great Horseshoe patron, Hamish McAlpine, scion of the English building dynasty.

Quigley also took the marriage service when Reggie Hastings married Kate Braithwaite, whose father, Sir Roderick, had been British ambassador in Moscow. When Quigley found out that there were Russians in the church, he broke into fluent Russian.

Guinness

Guinness is the lifeblood of Dublin and the Liffey is the lifeblood of Guinness. Together, they make up the lifeblood of the country. I was first introduced to the Guinness brewery as a small child when we went to Dublin on our holidays. My uncle, John Brennan, had a pub called the Harbour Lights Bar in the shadow of the brewery at 6 Echlin Street. He served the men of the brewery for over thirty-six years in his pub. In those days, in the 1950s, Guinness had a grain train that ran around the outside of the brewery and, as kids, we would ambush the train playing cowboys and indians. Brendan Grace was one of the young lads who played with us in those days, long before he became famous.

My mother had an uncle, Paddy Grant, who also worked for Guinness. He was a member of the crew on the Liffey bog boats. An aunt of mine also married a Guinness man and I often heard them talk of the benefits of working for Guinness, the medical care and housing – indeed, it was said that you could be born and buried by Guinness. That is how well the company looked after its people. The Guinness family were very good to the people of Dublin. They gave them the Iveagh Market in Frances Street, the Iveagh flats in Patrick Street and the Iveagh Hostel. Not to forget St Stephen's Green and Iveagh House, now the Department of Foreign Affairs. Both of these institutions were gifts of the Guinness family to the people of Ireland.

When I was about fourteen years old, I travelled on a CIÉ barge – the 52M – along the Grand Canal from the harbour on James's Street to Carrick-on-Shannon. It was loaded with Guinness barrels. It was a wonderful trip.

In 1959, I went to serve my time in the Harbour Lights Bar and served many a Guinness man. That same year, I was invited to the 200th Guinness birthday party by one of my customers, Mick Delahunty. It was a wonderful experience, with a huge fireworks display. In 1961, I left Dublin and went back home to Belfast to work for the Irish Bonding Company, which later became part of the Guinness Group. I worked in White's Tavern Wine Cellar Entry in Belfast and served the first bottles of Harp Lager, when it was new to the market. In 1963, John Lavery, then the MD of Guinness Northern Ireland, offered me a job as a rep for the company but I turned it down. I did think about taking it but, instead, I arrived back in Dublin in 1974.

When I was managing the Horseshoe Bar, our draught beers were two taps of Guinness, one of Harp, one of Carlsberg, one of Heineken and one of Smithwicks. I was approached on several occasions to replace the Harp for another lager but always said no. While I was running the Horseshoe, Harp would always be served.

The only difference between the Horseshoe and bars in Las Vegas was the Horseshoe had a clock – and it was a Guinness clock! In 2001, I took a month-long holiday in Australia and, on my first day back to work, I noticed the clock had been replaced by one with another brand name. To make matters worse, the Harp had also been replaced with another lager. I immediately called Guinness service and asked then to have the Harp tap restored and I got on to Guinness merchandising for a clock. The clock I was looking for was not easy to find. It was a round clock with the Guinness name in the centre. They sent me out a few other clocks but none of them would do. I pleaded with the merchandisers, explaining my predicament and asking them to find me one of the old clocks. True to form, Guinness did not let me down and I got an original one. They said that, one day, they would tell me where they got it. I found out but I will never tell. I will only say that one is missing in the display cabinet in the Guinness Hop Store.

In 1994, I was sent to Abu Dhabi to oversee the setting up of the first Irish bar in the Forte Grand Hotel, and to teach the staff how to pour a pint of Guinness and to make an Irish Coffee. I set to work getting the Guinness equipment in place and, to my horror, realised that the glasses I was sent were all shapes and sizes. I made it very clear that Guinness could not be served out of them. I immediately got in touch with the agent in Dubai and insisted that we were sent Guinness pint and half-pint glasses. I told him to get in touch with London or Dublin immediately and have them send me out the glasses I needed. I knew that they would not let me down and the glasses arrived two days later.

On the opening night of the bar, I was told at the last minute that I was to give a talk on the Black Stuff. I was to speak to the invited guests of which there were about 200. One of the guests was Paul Carthy, who is now in charge of the wonderful experience that is the Guinness Storehouse. I gave a brief history of Guinness and finished up by saying when you have given blood in Ireland, you get a glass of Guinness to get your strength back and when a woman has given birth in Ireland, she is rewarded with a pint of Guinness. I reminded them that Guinness is one of the largest breweries in the world selling over 7 million pints a day. I also mentioned some of the people I had had the great pleasure of serving of the years, including Lord Iveagh, Lord Moyne, Oonagh Guinness, Gareth Browne, whose grandfather was Ernest Guinness, Kim Kindersley and many other members of the Guinness family.

Today, in 2009, I am celebrating fifty years as a barman and Guinness is celebrating 250 years of brewing – and I am still serving Guinness.

P.J.

I first met P.J. Mara in 1989 when he was the government press secretary and closely associated with the rise of C.J. Haughey. In those days, P.J. was a very prominent person in Irish political life and people liked to be in his presence. Those who did not know P.J. would soon find out that he was a very private person who enjoyed a drink with his friends and did not like to be disturbed or stared at. Sadly, this was impossible to avoid considering the position he had.

On a Friday at about 5 p.m., you would find P.J. holding court in Horseshoe as only P.J. could. Some of his friends, like Sam Smyth and Tim Ryan and other newspapermen, would be listening to every word and watching for the expressions on his face to see if there was a story in what he was saying. If P.J. wanted to tell a journalist a story, he could do it without words. On such occasions, the staff knew not to bother him. I always knew when he was finished as he would smile at me and say 'a small Paddy, Sean', and make a retreat to the table in the corner with his friends. P.J. and his wife, Breda – and sometimes his son, John – would have afternoon tea in the Lord Mayor's Lounge. The Unicorn restaurant on Merrion Row was his usual haunt for Saturday lunch. It was not easy to get a table there, but P.J. always managed. He was one of the last customers to have a drink with me on the eve of our closing on a Holy Thursday night. He called in at about 1 a.m. on a Good Friday morning to say goodbye. I was very pleased to see him and asked him to have a drink. He reminded me that it was Good Friday and it was against the law to serve alcohol. I said, 'To hell with it! We are going to have one last drink in the Shelbourne as we know it.' P.J. had his usual Paddy and I had a Diet Coke. Since I left the Shelbourne, P.J. has kept in touch.

Bono

Bono graced the Horseshoe on occasion accompanied by Guggi, a famous painter in his own right whose paintings are in great demand. He was also sometimes with Simon Carmody, a musician, songwriter and long-time customer in the Horseshoe and also a good friend, and not to forget another of the boys, Gavin Friday.

We had a discussion on evening about the movie *The Gangs of New York* and the group's Oscar-nominated song 'The Hands that Built America'. Bono was very interested in that period in New York history and mentioned a scene at the dockside had left a lasting impression on him. It depicted young, Irish immigrant men just off the ships being forced to enlist in the Union army fight to in the Civil War. They were forced to board ships bound for the frontline in the shadow of coffins being unloaded. A few days later, I was listening to *Morning Ireland* presented by David Hanly. He was discussing a book called *Banished Children of Eve* by Peter Quinn giving the real story of *The Gangs of New York*. I asked a friend of mine, Stephen Stokes, of Stokes Bookshop George's Street Arcade, to find the book for me. I knew if anyone could find it he could and, indeed, he did.

Some time later, I was at the famous fiftieth-plus birthday for Oliver Caffrey in the south of France, which had a guest list that was a 'who's who' of Dublin and included Bono. I told him about the book and he was very taken with the title. When I got back in Dublin, I parcelled up to book and left it in with Principal Management at St John Rogerson's Quay. I had not heard from Bono if he had received the book, so I asked Simon Carmody, but he did not know. Sometime later, I met Bono and asked if he had enjoyed the book. He told me he had never received it, but that he would look into it. I still do not know to this day whether he ever got it or not.

The Lord Mayor's Lounge

No book about the Shelbourne would be complete without a mention of The Lord Mayor's Lounge. Elizabeth O'Neill and her fantastic staff – Maureen Crampton, Niamh Anderson and her sister, Claire, Hazel Anderson, Claudine, Daphna Cuddy, Catherine Conditer, Marie Nelson, Fiona Murphy, Emma Bradely, Audrey Bradley and numerous others over the years. You will find many of these girls working in top jobs in hospitality today. The Lounge is a hive of social activity for 'the ladies who lunch lightly' and for discrete businessmen who dare not risk the more confined space of the Horseshoe when conducting affairs public or private. It was named after the various Lord Mayors of the capital. For many years, its gracious environs were complimented by the gentle piano music played by Marie Whelan, who was well into her eighties.

The Master

John Cooney, journalist and author, is the director of the Humbert Summer School, which takes place in Ballina, Killala, County Mayo, in the last week of August and I am also a regular attender and look after Mr Cooney, Tony McGarry and the patrons of the school, when I'm there. The school takes its name from General Jean Joseph Humbert, the French general who landed in Killala Bay in 1798 to support the United Irishmen's rising against the British. I remember hearing U2 manager Paul McGuinness say 'be careful of Cooney because he will inform you that you are on the speakers list for this year's Humbert Summer School' – and he meant it. No one ever refused the invitation to speak. It is an honour to be included amongst the many names that have spoken over the twenty-odd years the school has been in existence. Those who have attended and spoken include: former president Mary Robinson (the school takes place in her home town); Llewellyn King, publisher of the Whitehouse Weekly; former Taoisigh, Gareth FitzGerald and Bertie Ahern; U2's manager, Paul McGuinness; P.J. Mara, former government press secretary; Cyril Kelly, former High Court judge; David Trimble, former leader of the Ulster Unionist Party; and John Hume, who shared the 1998 Nobel Peace Prize with Trimble; Gerry Adams and Martin McGuinness of Sinn Féin; journalist and press secretary, Bill Heeney of the Scottish Assembly; Alex Salmond, speaker of the Scottish Assembly; and Paul Gillespie.

Cooney was a Horseshoe Bar habitué and ran many of his campaigns from there. His clipped Glaswegian tones echoed over the bar counter as he expounded on matters of Church and state into the wee hours. His biography of Archbishop John Charles McQuaid was considered a masterpiece.

The Cheques

Cheques were a no—no for the Horseshoe Bar – Angela O'Connor in accounts would not accept them in the end-of-day cash.

I remember one particular gentleman who was wrongly accused, when approached by a member of staff, about a cheque being returned. He was in the company of a very accomplished journalist when a prominent lawyer addressed the Friday-night crowd. He said, 'I have been accused of writing a cheque that was not honoured. It is not true, you are all my witnesses, I have been slandered. I except to own the hotel when my action has been settled, so I am buying you all a drink on the house!'

Member of the House

One evening, we were honoured with a visit from Bob Reno. I think he was a journalist and good friend of Sam Smyth's. Bob is the brother of a former US attorney general. When he saw the Horseshoe and its crowd, he said, 'You would have to go outside to change your mind.'

The Cubs of the Tiger

Back in the early 1990s, many young men and women from all walks of life headed for the capital. It was not long before they discovered that the Horseshoe Bar on a Friday night was the place to be seen. There were contacts to be made for the young Turks with ideas and little money. In those days, it was a pint of beer and a glass of wine, and, as years passed, it became a bottle of champagne and beautiful women.

Monday to Wednesday were normal days, well as normal as can be in the Horseshoe. Thursday's late-night shopping would have the bar thronged with all of the beautiful ladies fresh from shopping at Grafton Street's Brown Thomas, Switzers and Richard Allen. But Friday night was the magical night. Business men and women would meet in the bar which would be packed to capacity and the champagne would flow like water. 'A place where men with no future met women with a past', is how the legend goes and they were all there in droves. The bar was so busy that they would spill out into the lobby. We would have six bar staff and two glass washers on duty. One Friday night, the phone rang, it was Paul McGuinness calling from the porter's desk to place an order which was promptly served.

On Friday nights, you would find yourself in the presence of builders, contractors, surveyors, subcontractors, architects, bankers and building society mangers and, of course, the solicitors and barristers who would cement whatever contracts were made. You would see men breaking off into groups of twos and threes to make deals, and the shake of a hand would tell you the deal was done. The Shelbourne was the kind of a place that if it happened there, it was not long before you would hear about it as fact.

The Blackout

One night, we had a blackout and the Shelbourne was in the dark. We are on the same electrical link as Leinster House. Work was being carried out on Kildare Street and a JCB had cut through the cable. The bar was quiet that night and we put candles on the tables. Sometime later, we got word that the power would not be back and we had to close the bar. All but two people left: Eamon Dunphy and Liam Brady. Eamon refused to leave. I was not going to argue with him, so I put out a few bottles of Becks for Eamon and a few large whiskies for Liam, and left them to themselves. I did look in from time to time to see that they were not at each other's throats and, of course, they weren't. I'm only joking…

The Man with the Toolbox

Jim Bonnyman arrived into the Horseshoe and immediately made an impact. No one knew where he came from or what he was doing in Dublin. Some said he had won the English lottery, others said he had sold his business… who knows? He was a nice guy, very tall, very loud and boy could he drink. He had his own cocktail called a toolbox. It had everything in it! What was required was one large water jug filled with ice, three glasses of white wine, three glasses of red wine, two large vodkas, two gins, two whiskies and a glass of brandy! A squeeze of one large orange and then top off with cider and a slice of fruit. It was then stirred and served – and it was lethal. I only made it once or twice on special occasions.

Kiefer Sutherland

Actor Kiefer Sutherland and Kim Kindersley were good friends. Kim is the nephew of Gareth Browne of Luggala, County Wicklow. I first met Kiefer a few weeks after Julia Roberts had left him, and Kim had come to stay with us in the Shelbourne. Both Kim and Kiefer were great characters. Kiefer stayed with us most weekends when he was working on the *The Three Musketeers*. He took a great shine to my daughter, Etain, and would ask if he could take her back to LA. I said, 'That's up to Etain.' He introduced her to some of his friends in the film business. Sometime later, she was asked to go for a screen test for the Mel Gibson film *Braveheart*. She got the part, but decided to take her place in Cardiff University instead.

Sinead O'Connor

When staying in the hotel, Sinead O'Connor would stroll through the lobby barefoot to the sheer horror of management. She was at the height of her international stardom at the time and always caused a stir in the hotel though, like many stars who frequented the place, she kept very much to herself.

The Poet

John McNamee is one of the most underrated poets in Ireland, but he was the bane of my life. He would arrive into the Horseshoe in his sheepskin coat and fedora hat, smoking a cigarette and was always heard before he was seen. He had such a hearty laugh. He always had a book, a CD or a single sheet of his latest poems in his possession.

Eventually, I had to bar him, but this did not stop him coming in. Any cigarettes that were left behind in the bar I would keep for him. I felt sorry for him as he was street poet. He had a great talent and toured America on several occasions and was sponsored by Bank of Ireland, amongst many others, including P.J. Mara and Noel Pearson. I arrived home late from work one night, turned on the television and there he was, with his trousers around his ankles sitting on a toilet bowl reciting his poetry!

> *'Wintered'*
> *Wintered city streets filled with a gawk of bad weather,*
> *As it upturns unwelcome showers of dislike on the rooftops,*
> *A cacophony only for the wise to navigate towards spring,*
> *A tension of the soul to bridge the season's rotary wheels of*
> *   solitude*
> *This night with its phlegmatic cough barking for some relief,*
> *Like Asia resting on the seashore of some desperation,*
> *The Human hulk of winter's passenger ship slowly noses the*
> *   ocean*
> *A galleon plodding in the regular rhythm of its sailors walk,*
> *The long haul on a sentinel's cold night, to once again hear*
> *A blackbird sings out loud.*
>
>

John McNamee
am 19 January 2005
>

Rugby

Rugby was always a very important part of the hotel calendar. Rugby weekends were legendary. I first started working in the Shelbourne on a rugby weekend – and what a weekend it was. It was decided to turn the Lord Mayor's Lounge into a bar. All the furniture, and even the carpet, was removed and the floor was protected with a temporary covering. We placed an eighteen-foot bar along one of the windows and had two service areas. Operating with two shifts, service stared at 7 p.m. on the Thursday and we closed at 4 a.m. the following Sunday morning. It worked very well.

In those days, the Irish team stayed in the Shelbourne and I hear that they have returned after a few years' absence.

The after-match dinner for the teams and IRFU personnel and guests was in the Ballroom. There was a two-tier system with wives and girlfriends dining on the first floor – the sort of segregation that could not happen today, but those were different times.

The Irish team would leave by bus to Lansdowne Road on a Saturday afternoon and would have to stop off at O'Donoghue's to pick up a few strays and Dessie

Hynes who would be there to wave them off. Win or lose, the Shelbourne buzzed with excitement, the bars were packed to capacity and the place was filled with excitement. When Wales were playing, the Welsh fans would sing long into the night. You saw the same faces, be they friend or foe, every second year.

Sunday morning saw me in the bar making jugs of Bloody Marys that were gone as soon as they were made. The Sunday papers littered the bar and the game was dissected bit by bit, it was all in good humour. The Scots were always very colourful in their kilts. The women, and some men, wondered what the Scotsmen wore under those kilts. I remember one year when Scotland played and it was very severe weather and it was touch and go whether the game would go on – but it did. On the Sunday, the weather became worse again and all sea and air travel was cancelled. This was another busy Sunday for the hotel, before everyone returned home in the early hours of Monday morning. The English were the big spenders. They arrived in groups, all members of rugby clubs, mainly men with very few women. The French on the other hand were no good to a bar, restaurants, yes, and shops like Brown Thomas where they spent a lot of money.

A few years ago, I recall standing on the North Circular Road at Russell Street waiting for my son, Daragh, who had tickets for the Heineken semi-final between Leinster and Munster. I noticed a lad standing next to me holding a card. It said he was looking for a ticket for the match. It reminded me of a day one rugby weekend when the bar was emptying out and everyone was heading for Lansdowne Road. This fellow handed me and envelope with tickets in it and said that someone would call for them. When he was about to leave, he turned and told me that if his friend did not collect the tickets, he would expect to see them there when he returned after the match. I took the envelope handed it back to him and told him to give them to his friends himself.

The Oil Baron and the Ferrari

John McKeown is an entrepreneur, financier and oil baron who stayed at the Shelbourne for his Christmas and New Year holiday. He always stayed in the Princess Grace Suite and, of course, always had his beloved slate-grey Ferarri 355 parked outside. It was usually parked in front of the hotel and was then moved overnight to the garage on Kildare Street. That was the responsibility of the night porters. On New Year's Eve, the night manager was David Moore O'Farrell and he was a great admirer of a Ferrari – we all knew he was looking for any excuse to drive one. When one of the porters told him that he was going out to park the car, David grabbed his chance and said that he would do it. The porter reminded him that it was not his job to park the cars. Moore O'Farrell quickly told him that, now, it was and the porter handed over the keys. Moore O'Farrell jumped into the car and roared off. Within minutes, he had lost control of the car and crashed into one of the grey pillars in front of St Stephen's Green. Luckily for him, he was not injured, just badly shaken. I'm sure he was concerned how he would explain the fiasco.

When he arrived back at the hotel, he said the car had hit black ice. One of the porters went out on to the road and said that he could not find any. A taxi driver was picking up a fare at Renard's nightclub and happened to tell Robbie Fox, the club's proprietor, about a Ferrari wrapped around a pillar outside St Stephen's Green. Robbie knew at once who owned the car and went into the club to find John to ask if he had parked his car at the Shelbourne. Robbie then told him what had happened. When John arrived back at the hotel, he asked where the car was and if anyone had been injured. He was assured that no one had been and was he was relieved to hear that. He said that the car was insured and can be fixed. When he arrived back from looking at the car, he said that the driver had been very lucky. Moore O'Farrell was very lucky that he did not lose his job. The Shelbourne management were not so lucky when they received the insurance bill.

The Irish-Canadian

An Irish-Canadian from Toronto with ancestors from Glencolmcille in County Donegal arrived in the Horseshoe one evening and met with James Craig. They immediately became very good buddies. The Canadian was interested in looking for investors for a new venture that he was setting up later that year. This was his reason for being in Dublin. James and the Canadian found that they had a lot in common. The Canadian had a great interest in young people and wanted to set up a trust, a scholarship of sorts, for young Catholics and Protestants in the North. It was intended that a pupil from a Protestant school in Belfast would exchange with a Catholic boy from St Coleman's in Derry. James was an old boy from Instonians in Belfast and the Canadian's family were ex-pupils of Instonians. James went to

Belfast to speak with the principal of the college and the Canadian did the same. The Canadian was to set up a fund for the exchange, which would last one year, though, if successful, it would be repeated year after year.

There was great publicity about this exchange as it was around the time of the Good Friday Agreement. It was something new and the schools embraced it willingly. As time went by, James became concerned as nothing was happening about the scholarship. The Canadian was back in Canada setting it up, but there was always an excuse for the delay and nothing ever happened. It was a terrible shame.

The Canadian had not been seen for about a year or so until, one day, he arrived back in the bar as bold as brass as if nothing had happened. James welcomed him with open arms and all was forgiven. James spent a weekend in Glencolmcille with him and his wife and, by all accounts, it went very well. It wasn't long before a new scheme was to be put in place. The Canadian was clever, he knew James could introduce him to the right people for an investment fund to be set up.

James introduced him to a managed fund accountant and a top solicitor to fund the investment. The company was launched with great excitement in the Merrion Hotel and no expense was spared. However, it was not long before investors started to worry. When the Canadian returned to Canada, a lot of people lost a lot of money. This was one of the less profitable ventures dreamed up in the Horseshoe Bar.

James Craig

It was said of James Craig that when he bought a suit, it was always a good one. He was always immaculately dressed at all times and was a man of many parts. He would break a £20 note on Monday and would still have change on Friday night. James' day started in the Lord Mayor's Lounge with breakfast of coffee and toast. Elizabeth O'Neill, manageress of the Lounge, was very good to him. When the Horseshoe opened, he was invariably first in. Tanqueray and tonic in a tall, stemmed glass and a Dunhill was his first order of the day. Out came the little tattered notebook held together with elastic bands. In this, he checked his itinerary for the day.

In his early days, when he graduated from college, his sister gave him a ticket on the *Queen Mary* to the US where he made a name for himself. He played a bit part on the Lucille Ball show *I Love Lucy*, which was a very big gig at the time. He had many other adventures in Los Angeles before returning to Ireland some time in the mid-1950s to try his hand at advertising, and he was quite successful.

One of his prize possessions was his Sunbeam sports car which was permanently parked outside the Shelbourne. His residence at that time was the Friendly Brothers of St Patrick Club in St Stephen's Green. When he was away on business, his Deluxe Sunbeam was parked in the club's car park. The club at one time asked him to find a new parking place as they needed the space he used. A friend of his volunteered a spot at his home in Malahide so the car went to Malahide. James was away for several months and, on returning, went to collect the Sunbeam and it was nowhere to be found. The friend who was minding it did not know what had happened to the car but had reported it stolen. It never turned up again and James was devastated.

He then pushed his energy into another venture, Emmet's Irish Cream but lost out badly on that venture. He was involved with a co-op in Kilkenny and that folded too. Back to the States went James to recharge the batteries. It was not long before he was planning a new venture – he intended to make nests of tables with the coats of arms of Irish clans, he thought it would appeal to the Irish Diaspora in the States. The tables were to be made in Donegal but, again, this did not come to anything.

The next venture was gold mining in the Sperrin Mountains in County Tyrone, when I heard about it, it started bells ringing with me and I spoke to James. He assured me that his partner had all the papers and licences in place. Again, the company was looking for funding and, again, a group of people was put together. One of the investors, whom I knew, asked what I thought. I just answered that all that glitters is not gold. I knew of the mine that they were talking about. It was nine miles north of Omagh in County Tyrone and had a high grid and quality of gold, the only problem was the gold would have to be refined at source and you would not get planning permission for it. I explained to James that the Omagh council would not give permission for the necessary cyanide dams as there were too many streams and small rivers running into the Ban, one of the finest salmon rivers in the North. James assured me that all this was in hand and had been approved. The idea was that the gold would be used for wedding rings, replica Tara brooches, Ardagh chalices and other artefacts. As usual, this was his story and the gold still remains in the hills of Tyrone.

James moved on to his next business venture, Blake's Liqueur, a rather bland-tasting drink that I could not see making the top ten as James assured me it would. A Dublin footballer of old was the main man behind the product. Once again, a consortium was put in place to market the drink. The US was to be the launching place and James was dispatched to acquire the importing licences from the appropriate people. The negotiations went on for a very long time and it looked as though they would never get them. If they could not get the licence, they would have to rethink their position, so back to Dublin came James. Back entered our old friend the Canadian. He suggested that if they launched the drink in Canada and floated it on the Canadian stock exchange, every licensed premise in the country, by law, would have to stock the drink.

James was made chairman of Inishmore Company, the vehicle used for launching the drink. A plan was put in place, the company was floated on the Canadian stock exchange and had quite a few takers. On paper, things looked very good. The introduction on the market in Canada was to be held at a St Patrick's Day dinner organised by the Sons of St Patrick and the guest of honour was to be the Lord Mayor of Toronto – naturally Blake's Liqueur was to be the after-dinner drink. By all accounts, it was a very successful night and Blake's went down very well. Some of those who took shares in Inishmore were locked in for a year, others for less. Those who were in for less did very well. The first year of Blake's was a fantastic success. At the first company AGM, everyone was in jubilant mood. The meeting was held in the company's offices which were in Merrion Square. Lots of drink was handed around, but little of the forecasts for the following year. The meeting announced that they had acquired a Russian vodka and it was announced that as tequila was to become very scarce in the following years, they would set about acquiring a distillery in Mexico – everything looked very rosy. James told me that he was buying an apartment in the Old Sweepstakes Building in Ballsbridge and that he was a millionaire on paper. I had my reservations.

The following year was not a good one. The market had not taken off as the footballer had predicted and doom and gloom descended on the Horseshoe. Poor James, the credit card was the first to go and out came the tattered notebook to see where he would start again. Sanity had been restored to the Horseshoe and a few people were still around to remind James of what they had lost. The Dublin footballer I never saw again, he was probably looking for the tequila plants in Mexico.

Though James was getting on in years, the sparkle never left him and he was always trying something new. He visited his doctor when he was not feeling so good and the doctor told him to go easy on the drink. He allowed him one gin and tonic a day, or so James said. I kept him to that and was not very popular over it. He usually left the Horseshoe about lunch-time to go and eat and have a glass of wine in the Ely Restaurant. I reminded him of what the doctor had said, one drink per day! James corrected me and told me that it was one drink per day, nothing about a glass of wine. James enjoyed life to the full and had many friends, but sadly he died alone.

To end, I remember one night a little old lady well into her seventies arrived into the Horseshoe with bleach-blonde hair, ruby-red lips and immaculate nails wearing a fur coat to her four-inch stiletto heels. She made straight for the bar and climbed up on a stool. I let her settle herself. After a moment, I welcomed her to the Horseshoe and, with a broad New York accent, she said that she was glad to be there. She asked if I could make a very dry martini. I said, 'Yes, of course – with a twist or an olive? Coming up.' I presented the martini and waited for the verdict. She took out the olive and tasted the drink. She gave a wicked smile and said, 'Perfect.' I watched her for a while surveying the bar. She told me she was from New York and that this was her first visit. I said that I hoped she would enjoy her stay and not to hesitate to ask if she needed anything. She thanked me.

James was holding court at the other end of the bar, he had just found an old friend who was an ex-player from his favourite team, London Irish, and the drink was flowing. They were like long-lost brothers. The New York lady called me over and asked, 'Is that Jimmy Craig I see over there?'

'Yes that's Mr Craig,' I answered.

She just smiled. I watched her and she was watching James. After about ten minutes, she climbed down off of the stool and made her was over to where James was. She stood behind him and tapped him on the shoulder. She had to do it again and he responded by looking halfway around and, as she was small and with the crowd, he did not see her. Again, she tapped him on the shoulder. Getting annoyed, he turned quickly to see who it was. He stopped in his tracks when he saw her and after a few moments he said, 'Yes?'

She answered, 'Hello, Jimmy.'

He asked, 'Do I know you?'

'You should', came the answer.

'I'm sorry, I don't know *you*.' At that, he turned away.

Again she tapped him on the shoulder and he turned abruptly and asked, 'What is it?'

The little lady placed her two hands on her hips, 'You don't know me? You've lived in my house for the past three years.'

Before she could continue, he excused himself to go to the toilet and did not come back. The little lady returned to her stool and told me that James had stayed with her for a couple of years, sometimes the rent was on time and others it was late, but for all of that, she said he had a good heart. That was the reason for her being in the Shelbourne. He was always talking about the Horseshoe and she wanted to see it for herself.

Spooks in the House

Two gentlemen booked into the hotel. They spent their evenings drinking in the Horseshoe and it would not be an exaggeration to say that they stood out like sore thumbs. There was something not quite right about them and it was obvious to me that they were up to something. They parked three cars in the garage and drove them at different times of the day. The rumour around the front desk and garage was that they were SAS or MI6 out spying on the IRA. One of the garage attendants was quite worried about their activities, so he informed special branch that something was going on. One evening, special branch arrived and picked up these chaps. It turned out that they were working for an English 'red top' tabloid and were in Dublin investigating Chris de Burgh, trying to catch him with the children's nanny. This did not happen, so they left Dublin very quickly.

The Jeunesse Dorée

The Horseshoe always had a contingent of young people, most of whom were related to patrons of long standing. Many were Trinity students, including author Michael O'Sullivan who recalls how he and his friends made the Horseshoe a regular haunt when they were at the college. He remembers coming to the bar in the 1970s 'because it was then an oasis of calm in the heart of the city'.

During my own years there, I remember a glamorous young set of customers like Julian Pearson who was starting out on a career in international finance. He came in with his then girlfriend, now his wife, Gillian Mcnaughton, a member of one of Dublin's leading business families. There was the beautiful Zeynep Asya from an old Turkish diplomatic family, Joshua Morris-Lowe, a debonair, popo-playing, Trinity student whose capacity for quaffing Jameson whiskey was legendry. The crisp, upper-class, English accents of this set was reminiscent of the old days of Molly Cusack-Smith and the hunting blades of old Ireland. Presiding over this troupe of colourful characters was the Tom Driberg of his generation, James Gibbons, who, having left the novitiate at Glenstall Abbey, became an art dealer and later social diarist for the *Daily Mail*. I saw it as an inevitable progression for someone as quick-witted as he is and his bons mots would often do the round of the bar when he had settled in for a session with his friends, many of whom he addressed in his hallmark greeting, 'ave Darjeeling!'

Paul Ryan was part of this set, too. He abandoned a career in property in the south of France to take up a career in acting.

The Corrs

Andrea, of the famous Dundalk group The Corrs, was a regular in the Horseshoe. She was often in the company of Bono, Simon Carmody, Guggi and Gavin Friday. I found her a fascinating person, very friendly and chatty. Her brother, Jim, called me up one day and asked me to keep the bar open late for him and some of his friends. I would love to have done so but as the Horseshoe is a public bar, it had to abide by the licensing laws. I said that I was sorry but if he booked in we could serve him after hours as a resident, he declined. On the Holy Thursday night before we closed the Horseshoe when the hotel was being

My daughter, Etain, with Aidan Doyle, who can't believe his luck.

Alan Devlin, actor.

Film and theatre producer, Noel Pearson.

Michael O'Sullivan enjoying a quiet drink in the Horseshoe.

Ben Kylie relaxing with Eddie Linden.

Mick Mulcahy, painter.

The Hon. Gareth Browne and Michael O'Sullivan at Luggala in the late 1980s.

Sean with Eamon Dunphy.

Gerry Ryan.

The Horseshoe Bar entertained many international stars, including three of my favourites *(top)* John Hurt, with his wife Anwen Rees Meyers, *(above left)* Oliver Reed and *(above right)* Richard Harris.

The *Jeunesse Dorée*: *(Above)* social diarist
James Gibbons and *(right)* Gillian and Julian
Pearson.

The Horseshoe Bar was very popular with champagne drinkers – between 1998 and 2000, we had the largest sales of champagne in Ireland.

Sean Boyd, keeping an eye on things.

renovated, the Corrs and their father were there to say goodbye to a wonderful era in the history of the hotel and its staff.

Dessie Hynes

Dessie Hynes was the proprietor of O'Donoghue's in Merrion Row, one of Ireland's most famous bars. He was a wonderful character. When the lockout of the Shelbourne staff occurred in 1983, a friend of mine, former Fine Gael senator, Maurice Manning, got me a job in O'Donoghue's for three nights a week. That job saved my life. I remember one night a little after hours, a knock came to the door and someone said, 'The guards are outside.' Dessie reached into his pocket and took out his rosary beads and then told the barman to open the door. You must remember the bar was full of people and, as the guards came in, Dessie turned to them and said, 'Good, lads, you are right on time. We are on the middle of the Sorrowful Mysteries.'

The sergeant looked at Dessie, 'Never mind the Sorrowful Mysteries, get this bar cleared.'

I have just been listening to the legendary Dessie on RTÉ radio's conversations with Eamon Dunphy. He was talking about rugby and the great internationals of the past. He said that the Welsh were the best spenders, followed by the Scots and the English, but that the French were no good at all to a pub. In the Horseshoe, it was the English that were the number one spenders, followed by the Scots and the Welsh. He was right about the French, they spend nothing, and they even brought their own bread and onions.

1983 – The Great Lockout

The strike, or unofficial strike, started in the Paddock Bar when the head barman objected to management working behind the bar. He told them that if they did not withdraw from the bar, he would remove his staff. The management explained that they were only helping out because of the level of business that night. The management continued working and the head barman removed his staff. The management had no choice but to suspend him. Word of his suspension quickly spread throughout the hotel. The restaurant staff all walked out. There was a stand-off and management closed the hotel. Incidentally, the head barman went on holiday the next day – leaving his staff picketing on the street. The lockout lasted for sixteen weeks and the staff found themselves in a very sticky situation. No strike pay or social-welfare payments were forthcoming. The unions maintained that it was a lockout and the social welfare would not pay out for unofficial strikes.

With no pay at all, it was very hard to make ends meet. I had two children and a mortgage at this stage. Josephine, my wife, was being paid social welfare for herself and the children. I was lucky that Maurice Manning found me that job in O'Donoghue's for two, or sometimes three, nights a week. Dessie's kindness saved my life and my home. It was later in the lockout that social welfare decided to pay out for the staff. I, unfortunately, was not covered as someone had incorrectly informed the social welfare office that I was working full-time in O'Donogue's.

A meeting was called in Liberty Hall to discuss an offer that the hotel had made. Expectations were high. When the conditions of returning to work were explained, you could have heard a pin drop. There was an air of disbelief and disappointment. The staff made it very clear to our union representatives that this was a non-runner.

There were three main conditions on returning to work: redundancies would be offered but capped at eleven years' service; those who wanted to return to their jobs would have to reapply for them; and salaries would be between 10 and 15 per cent less than what had been earned before. The union made it very clear that there was no plan B.

The staff was very angry at the union for not fighting for its members. The union called for a vote on the proposal and it was rejected to a man. We were then told from the top table that this was the only offer available. Reject it and we were all out on the street and Forte would mothball the Shelbourne Hotel. They also reminded us that it was getting close to Christmas, a very effective scare tactic. In spite of this, the second vote was also rejected. One of the union members from the top table informed us that they were prepared to keep us there all night if necessary to try and get us back to work. After a long exhausting day of fighting and arguing with our union members and getting nowhere, reluctantly we took another vote in favour of returning to work. I felt that this was the end of the hotel union as we knew it.

I reapplied for my job at the Grill Bar and was told that it was closed and it would not be reopening. I was then informed that there was a job in Banqueting and I had no option but to apply. I discovered that my salary was £1,000 a year less than I had been earning before the lockout. I went to the union and asked what they could do for me. I was told, 'Fuck off you are lucky that you have a job.'

I was very upset and taken aback at his attitude. I thought about it for a day or two. I had been a union member all of my working life and my uncle, John Brennan, for whom I had worked early in my career, was a founding member of the Barman's Union of Ireland. It was very hard for me, but I resigned from the union. I was told that I would not work again in the hotel business. I went back to the Shelbourne and asked where I stood with them as I was no longer a union member. They informed me that the job was there if I wanted it. The union was not happy about this and informed management that I was not to be paid service charge.

Service charge is a very big part of your salary. It is paid by the guest on leaving the hotel for services rendered and it is divided out amongst the staff. Before the lockout, service charge was applied and divided out by department. With the return to work, the service charge was now divided out amongst all staff who worked in the hotel both front and back of house. The Shelbourne assured me that they would make up my service charge. Over the following weeks and months, more staff members resigned from the union. The unofficial strike cost the union 50 per cent of its hotel members and it never recovered.

It was said later that members of our staff and union who kept us up all night to end the strike had ulterior motives. Good jobs had been procured at a new hotel being opened shortly in the city centre. If the staff had rejected the offer and the hotel had closed, these people would have lost their redundancies and their well-paid jobs.

When the management of the hotel heard that we had accepted the offer, it was with disbelief. 'How could they have accepted such an offer?' said one member of the management. 'They must have known there would be a plan B.' Indeed, a plan B did exist which was to offer redundancies and to offer us the same rate that we went out at. The management of the Shelbourne celebrated long into the night in Buswell's Hotel, drinking champagne and not believing their luck.

The owner of the new hotel where some of the staff had gone to work was P.V. Doyle. He was heard to say that if he was to get the same deal as the Shelbourne he would be a very happy man.

Blood on the Carpet

Gerry Danaher, senior counsel, was a member of the state's legal team at the time of the Beef Tribunal. Adrian Hardiman, senior counsel, was acting for the PD leader Dessie O'Malley. It was business as usual on a Friday night in the Horseshoe Bar when Gerry got into an argument with Dermott McGuinness, who was junior counsel to Adrian Hardiman.

Really, it was more social banter than an argument. I knew this because of the way Danaher was acting, laughing and messing about. Danaher told McGuinness that the state's legal team had access to confidential documents concerning O'Malley, supplied to his office by Fianna Fáil. A later inquiry established that this was not true and that Danaher had made up the story. The Taoiseach at the time was Albert Reynolds and his coalition partner was Dessie O'Malley. The government finally fell apart, leaving the way clear for Bertie Ahern. The whole affair was blown out of all proportion. For weeks afterwards, people would ask where this confrontation took place. I think they were expecting to see blood on the carpet from the scars of this legendry legal skirmish.

A Man of Distinction

Simon Cummins was a man of distinction in the early 1990s. His trademark was a bottle of DP paid for on an American Express card. He was an entrepreneur of sorts. He had made a bid for the stage version of *The Rocky Horror Picture Show* and had secured it for himself and his partners. I remember the opening night well. It was a night filled with excitement and glitter and, of course, plenty of DP. Unfortunately, it did not last for very long. I think this was because of all of the free tickets and the lack of backing from the Arts Council.

Simon, being the man that he is, was back up on his feet in no time at all. He made a bid for no less than the Shelbourne itself! We were all aghast at the idea. A meeting with Rocco Forte, who then owned the hotel, was held in the Forte Airport Hotel with Simon and his advisors. Talks went on for a few days but nothing came of it. The price Simon offered was in the region of 17 million but it was not enough. After this, Simon was out on the road again and started up a taxi company – or so we were told. What we do know for certain is that he is out there doing what he is best known for – the entrepreneurial spirit.

Girls Behind the Bar

The Horseshoe from its conception was totally male oriented. The first job I had when I took over was to sort out the staff and to sort out a bit of female glamour. Such change was vigorously opposed by some members of staff and not a few customers. However, they were told that this change was going ahead whether they liked it or not. And so it did. The first to start was my own daughter, Etain, on a casual basis followed by Emma Beatty, Helen Hardy and Emma Bradley followed by many others over the years. They were always popular with the customers.

Three Blondes and a Funeral

Stan Gebler Davies was a friend to all who knew him, especially the *Sunday Independent* journalist, Brigid McLaughlin, with whom he was very close. Stan was a brilliant journalist and the only would-be politician who stood for the Unionist Party in his native Cork. Needless to say, he was not elected. He had columns in the *Telegraph*, *Mail* and *Express* the *Independent* in London and *The Spectator*, along with many other magazines. He loved his cigars and a glass of chardonnay.

Stan spent his day between the Horseshoe and Doheny & Nesbitts. Even though Stan had many friends, he was a lonely man. I met him late one night as I was on my way home. He was wandering around Baggott Street, seemingly lost. I stopped the car and asked if he was okay. I could see that he was not and offered him a lift home. He accepted and it was only then that I realised that he lived in Dalkey and I lived in Sutton, the other side of Dublin Bay, but Stan's need was greater than mine and off we set. Even though he was a little worse for wear from the drink, he was great company. He told me stories of evenings spent in

Oliver Caffrey's house in Kildare and evenings spent with Fr Sean Quigley. He could really tell a story and so it seemed like no time until we were in Dalkey. I had no problem finding his home. I dropped him off and saw that he got in safely. I then headed off for Sutton.

Stan came in the next day and thanked me for my kindness, I was only glad to see him home safe. It was not long after that evening that Stan died in a tragic accident that should never have happened. I was very upset because I liked Stan very much. His funeral was on a beautiful June day and the church in Dalkey was filled to overflowing. Everyone who was anyone was there. The priest was a good friend of Stan's, unfortunately I cannot remember his name. He spoke with great admiration and humour about Stan and, would you believe it, in the front pew were the three blondes in Stan's life, kneeling side by side, Brigid, Bee and Mary. I am sure that Stan was looking down and smiling at this. They buried Stan in great style. Back at the Queen's pub in Dalkey, the reception went well into the night and then into the next day. You could not expect anything less for such a man as this legend of old Fleet Street was. A few people attempted to drive home, but they ended up visiting the garda station as a result. Stan was cremated and the crematorium had to call the family to remind them to collect the ashes, which were to be scattered at sea – but that is another story for another day.

The Man from Riverdeep

I first met Barry O'Callaghan in the 1980s and as he was just starting at the university, he was looking for a part-time job. He is the son of a County Cork doctor and if he were less enterprising, he could have rested on his laurels and let the family pay his way. This, however, was not his style. There were not a lot of jobs going at that time of economic recession but he made a serious impression on me and I wanted to help him. I suggested a job in Banqueting. It carried long hours and the work was hard. He jumped at the opportunity.

When he got his first wage, which was on the basis of £5 an hour, plus service, he was overjoyed at his good fortune. Barry was with us through all his university years.

At that time, Banqueting had a great bar crew. John McGuirk, Derek Allen, Damien Foley and Paul Murphy, the son of our legendary head waiter Paddy

Murphy. There were three brothers, Rock, Sean and Pat Meehan. I christened them Rock One, Rock Two and Rock Three. They were also at university. Rock ended up working at Davy Stockbrokers, and Sean and Pat are in the medical profession. Timmy Spillane was the other legendary head waiter on the ballroom staff and his son and daughter, Gareth and Sinead, also worked there.

When Barry graduated, he left the Shelbourne and moved to bigger and better things. It always appeared to be his destiny to do something great. Barry worked in the States and in several other places before establishing one of the largest educational publishing empires in the world. Over the years of his rising success, he always called to see me in the Shelbourne whenever he was in town. If I was not there, he would leave his card. It was nice to know that he never forgot us.

He moved back to Dublin in the 1990s with a company called Riverdeep which he developed into a major international success. He arrived in the Horseshoe one night unexpectedly, and, as luck would have it, it was the Shelbourne's 175th birthday party. I insisted that he came as my guest to join the celebrations and he gracefully accepted. All the ladies who worked in the ballroom were delighted to see him as they had a soft spot for him. He launched Riverdeep on the Stock Exchange in March 2000. I bought a few shares and did very well from them. He was back in the Horseshoe with some friends one night and we had a great chat about old times.

As history has it, Barry went from up to down to back up again, you could not keep him down. I heard one day that a hotel where he spent many happy days during his school holidays was being demolished and replaced by an apartment block. Barry thought that Dungarvan in County Waterford should not lose a hotel of that standard. He made the developer an offer that he could not refuse; developed the hotel and turned it into a boutique hotel and modernised the marina. He did a fabulous job on transforming it.

Barry went on to develop his beloved Riverdeep whose shares later dropped from $50 to $20. He decided to buy back his company and start again. He went from strength to strength but reading the papers you would not believe it. They were very hard on him but he did not let that stop him. Barry went to the States and did one of the biggest deals ever negotiated by an Irishman.

The Fourth Estate

As a watering hole for the fourth estate, the Horseshoe Bar had no peer in the 1980s. Throughout the decade, many newspaper editors used the bar as a meeting place at one time or another. Aengus Fanning, one of the longest serving editors of the *Sunday Independent* was a regular, often meeting politicians or high-profile businessmen and combining a little leisure with a lot of hard work. Another visitor was Tom McGurk, a leading political and sports commentator. Others I recall include former RTÉ London correspondent Mike Burns and his colleague from radio, Gerry Ryan, who regularly visited with Bono and Paul McGuinness from U2. Tim Ryan, who wrote a bestselling biography of P.J. Mara, regularly met Mara in the bar for long chats. There were many press photographers who also used the bar regularly. Principally, John Moran, who had a distinguished Fleet Street career and is also well known for his art photography.

The Half-Pint of Guinness – Sayonara

One morning, just as I had finished preparing the bar for opening, having had breakfast with Betty O'Neill and Joe O'Reilly, the purchasing manager, I had barely opened the door when I was met with a rush of Japanese ladies armed with cameras heading into the Horseshoe Bar. They were chattering away to me in Japanese had I hadn't a clue what they wanted. At one stage, they got quite loud. I expected to find someone in charge of this wandering group but no one seemed to be in control and I got quite worried. I left the bar and went out to the Front Lobby to the porter's desk to find out where they had come from. Porter Noel Shane said that a bus pulled up outside and they all poured into the hotel. I went out to the bus to find the guide who was with them and see what was going on. The tour guide came with me into the bar and explained that they all wanted a pint of Guinness to have their photos taken with. I suggested that a glass (half-pint) would be more appropriate and it was agreed.

I set about pouring twenty half-pints of Guinness. When I had finished pouring, they all huddled into a group for the photograph. The cameras were being passed back and forth to make sure that all got a shot. The next thing I knew, they were not drinking the Guinness they just put them back on the bar and filed out the door bowing and smiling and saying, 'Sayonara', and piled back on to the bus. I was gobsmacked and went to find the tour guide to find out who was paying for the twenty half-pints of Guinness. She said they only wanted to have their photos taken with the Guinness but did not think that they had to pay. Wasn't I lucky that I didn't pour the pints? Lesson well learned. It was good fun and I can still hear the Japanese ladies bowing and smiling and saying, 'Sayonara.'

The Chairwoman

Gillian Bowler and Gerry Robinson frequented the Horseshoe upon occasion when Grenada owned the Shelbourne. She was then the owner of Budget Travel. In 1994, I booked a holiday with her company to Malta. It was a disaster. When booking, we asked for a quiet part of Malta but instead we were booked into a hotel on the main street in Valetta. Our room was just above a disco and the noise was so loud that a bottle of body lotion cracked down the middle from the vibration. If that was not bad enough, a building site was in full swing just across from the hotel with a pneumatic drill going constantly from 7 a.m. We were told that there was nothing that could be done about it. We found ourselves another, quieter hotel and moved in.

When we returned to Dublin, we made a complaint to Budget Travel and got nowhere. I decided to write to Gillian Bowler to explain my dissatisfaction with my holiday and the treatment received by her company. I asked if she could look into my complaint. I received a return letter explaining that she did not get involved in the day-to-day running of the business. I took my complaint to the tribunal and got nowhere. It was the only time in my long experience of Horseshoe Bar customers that one of them would not extend a small favour to me when politely asked.

Cowboys and Cowgirl

One cloudless morning, three Americans arrived at Dublin airport, collected their bags and headed for the door. They hailed a taxi and loaded up their bags.

The taxi driver asked, 'Where to?'

One of the gents said, 'To the best hotel in Dublin.'

The driver, without thought, said, 'The Shelbourne.'

They said, 'Drive on.'

The three booked in and eventually found their way to the Horseshoe where I was on duty. In they came, two gents and one lady, all dressed on cowboy boots Stetsons, checked shirts and jeans. I thought to myself, What am I in for now? They introduced themselves and asked where all of the action could be found. I told them about O'Donoghue's for a glimpse of Irish music and hospitality, suggested a trip to the Guinness brewery and the Irish Whiskey Corner. If they wished to see historical Dublin, I recommended a bus tour and in the evenings for dinner, McGrattan's in the lane, Dobbin's or the Unicorn and, of course, our own restaurant, No. 27. They looked at me and said they were sure they could find something from all of that.

I asked what they would like to drink and they asked what I recommended. I asked if it was their first visit to Ireland and they said it was. I told them that in that case there could only be one drink… Guinness.

They said, 'Okay, three glasses.'

'No, two pints and a glass for the lady to start,' I corrected.

They watched me with great interest as I poured two pints and a glass of Guinness. When the Guinness was ready, I told them that when they were drinking their Guinness, they should just think about what they are drinking, and not be too quick to give a verdict. I explained to the lady why I gave her a glass and not a pint, saying that, to her, a pint might look too much as she had never experienced Guinness before. I was right. For the next week, that they stayed with us, every time they came into the Horseshoe it was always 'three pints of Guinness, please'.

Cowboys and cowgirl they might have been, but they were very interesting people. They came from Reno, Nevada, and had a ranch the size of Ireland to which they keep adding. Every time land came on the market near the ranch, they bought it. The ranch has only one road and that is to the main house, the rest are only trails. They only transport they use are horses. Their main aim is to return the land as close as possible back to its natural state. The problem is to keep out four-wheel drives and quad bikes and to stop people from Reno trespassing on their ranch and destroying the habitat.

The two cowboys and the cowgirl were full of surprises. It turned out that they owned the oldest hotel and saloon in Reno, built just before the start of the US Civil War. It is the same today as it was the day it was built and that is the way they want to keep it. They are also attorneys-at-law, and not only that but they are also bounty hunters. They own one of the biggest companies in the US. They were something else.

After their week's stay, they asked me to recommend where they should go next. I recommended Limerick as I had a friend who had a hotel close to the Kingdom of Kerry, the beautiful west Cork and to the Cliffs of Moher. I rang Tom Kane in Adare Manor and asked if he could accommodate them. I put one of them on the phone and after a lengthy time, they struck a deal and off they went to stay in the Manor. They came back two or three weeks later and returned to the Shelbourne and could not stop talking about the beauty of the countryside and how well they were treated here. They loved Ireland and said that they would be back. The invited me to Reno with the promise to show me their country as I showed them mine. Myself and my friend, Arthur McCoy, were to go but, like some many things in life, we never got around to it. Maybe we will someday.

Marie and Des Carroll

Marie Carroll and her husband, Des, graced the Horseshoe of many an evening – she is easily recognised by the baseball cap she always wears, like a trademark. She is a very famous artist and one of her subjects is the Shelbourne. The old Shelbourne bar has appeared on many of her canvasses and the redhead Jenny appears behind the bar on many of them. Marie's paintings hang on the walls in the homes of many of Ireland's rich and famous. I myself have one of the Old Brown Thomas store on Grafton Street – now Marks & Spencers.

She loved to sit with Des at the bar of the Horseshoe, her enjoying a snipe of champagne and Des with a Bacardi and Coke. Des is also a very accomplished painter who specialises in landscapes. They both can be found displaying their works on St Stephen's Green on selected weekends and in the Apollo Art Gallery on the corner of Dawson Street and Duke Street in Dublin. It is a place to visit if only to browse and there is many a treasure and bargain to be found there.

Mary O'Carroll

Mary O'Carroll and many of her friends were regulars in the Horseshoe and the life and soul of many a party. The love of Mary's life is a beautiful little yoke, Sky – and boy was she spoiled. Every time you would see Sky, she had a new coat and not just any coat. Burberry, Gucci and Armani. Mary herself was no stranger to designer labels. One evening, the ladies arrived in their usual gaiety, Mary was carrying a larger bag than usual but I took no notice until I saw that the bag was getting a lot of attention. Eventually, I discovered a little head sitting out of the opening of the top of the bag. I called Mary aside and said, 'Mary, you know that here are no dogs allowed in the Horseshoe.'

She looked at me with those bog brown eyes and said, 'I couldn't leave her at home on her own.' Looking around the bar, she added, 'There are a couple of tow-legged dogs here already and no one is putting them out.'

I had to agree with her.

The Birthday Party

Over the years, many famous people from the world of sport could be found in the Horseshoe Bar. One was Alex Higgins a former world snooker player. One night, he was drinking with Eamon Dunphy. In the course of the evening, they were joined by Ronnie Woods of the Rolling Stones. Ronnie was having a birthday party at his home in County Kildare that night and invited Alex to come along. Alex was not sure, so Ronnie wrote down his address and gave it to him in case he changed his mind.

It was about 11 p.m. and, at this time, Alex was on his own. I asked him if he was going to the party and he couldn't make up his mind. I watched as he took out the piece of paper with Ronnie's address, he got up from his stool with the address in his hand and finished his drink and headed for the door. I watched as he left the hotel and hailed a taxi. He handed the address to the taxi driver and off they went.

It was pitch black by the time they arrived at the address at County Kildare. The taxi man pointed out the house. I'm not sure what happened next but Alex walked in the opposite direction in the pitch black and got lost. He was walking for quite a while, when he saw a light in the distance and made his way towards it. He made his way to the house, knocked at the door and waited. Eventually, an upstairs window was opened and a voice asked who was there and what was wrong. Alex said that he as looking for Ronnie Wood's house, a voice answered, 'You are a long way from there.' The man at the window asked, 'Would that be Alex Higgins?'

'It is,' answered Alex, 'and I am lost. How can I get to Ronnie's house?'

The voice answered, I will be down in a minute and I will take you. Alex was delighted and thought that he was on the pig's back. The man arrived from the gate at the side of the house pushing a bicycle. Alex looked in amazement and the man said hop up on the bar. That is how Alex Higgins arrived at the birthday party at Ronnie Wood's house – it's a story he tells himself.

The Bow and Arrow

Brian Archer has led an incredible life. People wonder how he is still around today. He was a king in the rag trade, a financial trader (he was lucky he was never caught… only kidding) a nightclub boss, owned a car-valeting service and was a runner for a leading restaurant. One day, he was up, the next day, he was down – and it did not matter, because Brain always landed on his feet. He was also a big hit with the ladies. His best friend is Louis Murray of La Stampa restaurant. Louis, himself, runs his own hotels, bars and nightclubs in Dublin, but, nowadays, spends much of his time in Spain playing golf with his friends.

Getting back to Brian, he could be difficult at times, especially after a few drinks. There was one particular lady in his life we will call her Maid Marion, and the friction between them could be electrifying. It became so bad one evening that I told him that if he wanted to drink in the Horseshoe, he would have to do so in his own and that Maid Marion could go to the Shelbourne Bar. The two faced each other so they could wave to one another across the Lobby. Brain is leading a much quieter life today. A long-time customer in the Lord Mayor's Lounge, Davy Byrne would say about Brain, 'He was the cleverest man in Dublin. He never did a day's work in his life.'

Prince of Darkness

Aidan Doyle is one of the last great managers of the 'hotel' business. His working life spanned many decades – too many for me or anyone else to count. He spent many of those years working for the Doyle group of hotels. The Berekeley Court, The Burlington including, of course, Anabel's nightclub, where he earned the title, 'the prince of darkness'.

One Friday night, he was at his usual spot in the Horseshoe Bar, having his customary scotch and Diet Coke and smoking a large, Havana cigar. That was his trademark. A very irate lady approached him. She asked if he was the manager. Aidan, being Aidan, said that he was. She then went into a litany of complaints. This took him completely by surprise. Poor Aidan had met his match and this lady was not for stopping.

Eventually, he put his hand on her shoulder and said, 'You have my deepest sympathies, I'll tell you what to do. Tomorrow morning, ring the hotel and ask for the duty manager, and tell him what you have told me. I assure you that he will handle your complaint.'

The lady left with that assurance. Aidan turned to me and asked, 'What was that all about?'

I said to him. 'Look at your lapel.'

He looked and there was his name badge, 'Aidan Doyle, Manager'. He apologised to me and took it off. I set him up a drink on the house, I think that he'd earned it.

Chapter Five

Cocktails

T HE DEFINITION OF a cocktail, according to the Oxford English Dictionary, is:

1. an alcoholic drink consisting of spirit mixed with another drink such as fruit juice relating to or associated to cocktail drinking or formal social occasions or a cocktail dress.

2. a dish consisting of small pieces of food typically served as an hors d'oeuvres or prawn cocktail.

3. a mixture of substances of factors especially when dangerously or unprecedented a potion or cocktail of drugs.

The Origin of the Cocktail

It was said to denote the horse with a docked tail. Later, it was a racehorse that was not a thoroughbred because of a cocktail horse in its pedigree.

Of course, there are other stories and definition for the cocktail. A lot of people thought that the name came from the Americas, but it was known long before America was 'discovered'. Harry Craddock has his own version of the origins of the cocktail as published in January 1936 in *The Bartender*, it is as follows:

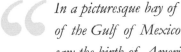
In a picturesque bay of the peninsula of Yucatan and washed by the waters of the Gulf of Mexico lies the historical port of Campeche, that in its time saw the birth of America's most daring sailors and cleverest shipbuilders.

Many years ago noble English sailing vessels arrived at this tropical port to take in cargoes of mahogany and other precious woods and many other products.

The English officers and sailors went ashore to visit the port and contemplate the ruins of the fortifications that in former times had defended the town against the pirates, some of whom reached the high rank of admiral in the Armada of Her Majesty, the Virgin Queen. They quenched their thirst at the doors of taverns in the narrow streets of the city or under the deep arches of the main square. In those times, wine liqueurs and strong alcoholic drinks were drunk without mixing. But in this particular part of the world, drinks were sometimes ordered which were called 'dracs' of brandy, rum or some other alcoholic ingredients. These were mixed drinks prepared in a thick, coarse glass slowly stirred with a spoon. The word drac was probably a corruption of Drake, the British hero adventurer of the high seas.

In one of these taverns in the picturesque Mexican port, shaded by the graceful palms and perfumed by the sea breeze and the scent of sandalwood from the forests, the boy who served the drinks, instead of a spoon used the fine slender root of the plant which, owing it's peculiar shape was called 'cola del gallo', which in English means 'cock's tail'. The English sailors who became accustomed to drink dracs, upon seeing the boy mixing them with this root, which to them would have seemed very strange, asked what it was and the reply was 'Cola del Gallo' or in English 'cock's tail'.

Soon, the word with which they had baptised the drinks of that port, mixed with the famous root became common among sailors landing in Campeche, nobody ordered 'dracs' but only 'cock tails'.

The English sailors soon made the new name very popular in the taverns in the port of the British Isles where it passed on to the bars along the piers in the ports of the United States, and later to the whole world. Then came the fever for mixed drinks – The 'cock tails' became numerous and the 'cocktail shaker was born'.

That is one story – others probably better known include that of 'Xoc-tl', the daughter of a Mexican king, who served drinks to visiting American officers during a conference with her father. The Americans, approving of the drink and later introducing it at home, named it 'cocktail' after the king's daughter, this being the closest approximation to her name in English. And then also there is the story of Betsy Flanagan, tavern keeper in America in pre-Civil War days, who was said to have mixed drinks to her own recipe and these became known as 'cock's tails' owing to an escapade in which she and others were involved.

The Guild is of the opinion that it will always be a matter of conjecture as to the origin of the term 'cocktail' as we know it; one claim appears to be as fantastic as the other where drinks are mixed.

W.C. Fields (1880–1946), the famous American actor of stage and screen, had a great weakness for the martini. It was said that, on film sets, he had a flask of martini for medicinal purposes. One evening, he walked into a cocktail bar in Los Angeles and ordered a dry martini from the bartender. He watched the bartender place a frosted martini glass on a napkin on the bar. He then took a mixing glass and filled it three quarters with ice. He poured a generous measure of gin over the ice and then took the dry Vermouth bottle and, as if it were sniffing out the gin, knew exactly how much to put in. Not too little and not too much. This was all done in a ceremonial fashion. The right amount of Vermouth is the making of the martini. Taking a mixing spoon with a gentle stir the bartender mixed the contents together. He then withdrew the mixing spoon and tapped it gently against the side of the glass. Turning to a hawthorn strainer, he then placed it over the top of the mixing glass, lifted the glass with his right hand and placed his forefinger over the handle of the strainer and poured the martini into the chilled glass. He then placed a lemon in his left hand and with this right hand cut a thin sliver from the lemon about an inch long, placing the sliver between the forefinger and thumb of his left hand gently twisted the lemon over the martini. W.C., who was patiently watching this act of excellence, slowly looked up at the bartender and said, 'If had wanted a lemonade, I would have asked for a lemonade.'

The Home Bar

Essential Equipment

Corkscrew and bottle opener

Ice bucket and tongs

Silver tray

Shaker, standard or Boston type

Mixing glass, hawthorn strainer and bar spoon

Spirit measure

Fruit knife

Straws and cocktail sticks

Three glass cloths

Water jug

Glasses

Glasses work out at two glasses per person.

12 oz slim jims

Old-fashioned tumblers

Brandy glasses

Champagne flutes

It is a good idea for the host to have a different type of glass. Something with a little colour in it, because if you put it down, it will be easy to find. Always remember to have clear ice, as cloudy ice turns to water more quickly. The finishing touches to any party are to always serve potato chips and nibbles, such as olives, etc.

Cocktail List

Rosemantic

1967 Bisquit de Bouche All-Ireland Cocktail winner and my signature cocktail.

½ measure cognac
¼ measure Cointreau
¼ measure Cinzano Dry
¼ measure peach brandy

Add all the ingredients to a shaker. Shake and serve in a martini glass.

George Duffy's Salsa

George Duffy was the assistant manager of the Horseshoe Bar for many years. His cocktail salsa was placed fourth in the 1998 Havana Club, Grand Prix which took place in Cuba.

1 part white rum
1 part crème de banana
5 part pineapple juice
1 part cream shaken with an
added dash of grenadine

Put all the ingredients in a shaker and shake. Serve in a 12 oz slim jim glass and decorate with a strawberry and mint.

Irish Coffee

Stem glass
3 teaspoons of Demerara sugar
Strong black coffee
1 measure of Irish whiskey
Fresh double cream to taste
1 teaspoon
1 small plate with napkin

Heat an Irish coffee or stemmed glass and add three teaspoons of Demerara sugar, fill the glass three-quarters with black coffee. Add a half measure of Irish whiskey and stir in to dissolve the sugar. Pour the double cream using either the front or back of the spoon and float the cream over the top of the coffee. Place on a small plate with napkin and serve.

Bloody Mary

1½ measure Smirnoff vodka
Dash of fresh lemon juice
2 dashes of Tabasco
4 dashes of Worcestershire
   sauce
Dash of celery salt
Fill with tomato juice

Add all the ingredients to a shaker filled with ice. Shake together and strain into a tall glass filled with crushed ice. Garnish with a stick of celery. Some people like to add a dash of dry sherry. Note that this is a cocktail made for personal taste, some like it hot… so the quantities of Tabasco and Worchester sauce will vary.

Bull Shot

½ measure Smirnoff vodka
Dash of lemon juice
Dash of Tabasco
6 measures of cold consommé
   soup

Add all the ingredients to a shaker with ice. Shake and strain into a highball glass over crushed ice.

B52

½ measure Kahlua
½ measure Grand Marnier
½ measure Bailey's

Pour the Kahlua into a small shooter glass. Holding a cold teaspoon upside down (and only just touching the surface of the Kahlua) slowly pour the Grand Marnier over the back of the spoon to create the second layer. In the same way, pour the Bailey's over the back of a second spoon to form a third layer (the Bailey's, in fact, becomes the second layer, pushing the Grand Marnier to the top).

Cosmopolitan

¼ *measure Smirnoff vodka*
⅛ *measure Cointreau*
Dash of fresh lime juice
Dash of cranberry juice
Dash of crème de cassis

Add all the ingredients to a shaker with ice. Shake and strain into a chilled martini glass. Garnish with orange peel shaving.

To add a special touch, hold the shaving over a lighter for a few seconds to draw out the flavour, then add to the cocktail.

Galway Grey

¼ *measure Smirnoff vodka*
¼ *measure Cointreau*
Dash of brown crème de cacao

Place all the ingredients in mixing glass and stir. Serve in a martini glass with a float of fresh cream and a twist of orange.

Margarita

½ *measure white tequila*
¼ *measure Triple Sec*
Dash of fresh lime juice

Add all the ingredients to a shaker with ice. Shake together and serve in chilled margarita glass rimmed in salt. Garnish with a lime wedge.

Grasshopper

½ *measure green crème de menthe*
½ *measure white crème de cacao*
¼ *measure fresh cream*

Add all the ingredients to a shaker. Shake together and serve over cracked ice into a chilled martini glass with a straw.

Black Russian

½ *measure Smirnoff vodka*
½ *measure Kahlua*

Pour both ingredients into an old-fashioned glass filled with ice. Add Coke to make into a long drink.

Stinger

½ *measure brandy*
½ *measure white crème de menthe*

Add the ingredients to a shaker. Shake well and serve in a chilled martini glass.

Singapore Sling

½ *measure gin*
¼ *measure cherry brandy*
Dash of fresh lemon juice

Add all the ingredients to a shaker. Shake and serve in a chilled martini glass or over ice in an old-fashioned glass.

Mint Julep

5 sprigs of fresh mint
½ *teaspoon of fine sugar*
1 teaspoon of water
½ *measure bourbon*

Muddle together in a 12 oz glass until the mint flavour is extracted and the sugar has been dissolved. Add the bourbon. Serve in an old-fashioned glass filled with crushed ice. Garnish with a sprig of fresh mint.

Hot Whiskey

1 measure of Irish whiskey
2 teaspoons of sugar
Slice of lemon
4 cloves
Hot water

Heat a stemmed glass. Add the whiskey and the sugar to the glass and fill it with hot water. Garnish with a lemon slice studded with four cloves.

Tom Collins

½ measure gin
Dash of fresh lime juice
1 teaspoon of sugar
Dash of Angostura bitters
Soda water

In a shaker half-filled with ice cubes, combine the gin, lime juice and sugar. Shake well. Strain into a Collins glass almost filled with ice cubes. Add the soda water and bitters and stir.

Brandy Alexander

⅓ measure crème de caçao
⅓ measure brandy
½ measure fresh cream
¼ teaspoon fresh ground nutmeg

Add the brandy, crème de cacao and cream to a shaker half-filled with ice cubes. Shake well and strain into a chilled martini glass. Garnish with the nutmeg.

Bartender

¼ measure dry gin
¼ measure dry sherry
¼ measure Dubonnet
¼ measure dry Vermouth
Dash of Grand Marnier

Add the ingredients to a shaker filled with ice. Shake and strain into a chilled martini glass.

Between the Sheets

¹/₃ measure brandy

¹/₃ measure Bacardi rum

¹/₃ measure Cointreau

Dash of fresh lemon juice

Add the ingredients to a shaker. Shake and serve in an old-fashioned glass over ice.

Gibson

⁵/₆ measure dry gin

¹/₆ measure dry vermouth

Add the ingredients to a shaker half-filled with ice. Shake and strain in a chilled martini glass served with a pearl onion.

Gin/Brandy/Rum/Whiskey Sour

½ measure dry gin/brandy/ rum/whiskey

½ teaspoon of sugar

Dash of fresh lemon juice

Few drops of egg white

Soda water

Slice of lemon

Add the ingredients into a shaker. Shake and pour into a 12 oz slim jim glass. Top up with soda water and add a slice of lemon.

Seabreeze

½ measure Smirnoff vodka

6 measures cranberry juice

6 measures grapefruit juice

Pour the vodka into a 12 oz slim jim glass half-filled with ice. Fill partially with grapefruit juice and top with cranberry juice.

Horse's Neck

½ measure Cointreau

1 baby bottle of ginger ale

Rind of one lemon

2 sugar cubes soaked in
   Angostura bitters

Twist the rind of one lemon. Place it in the base of an old-fashioned glass and anchor with the sugar cubes soaked in Angostura bitters. Leave some of the lemon to curl over the lip of the glass. Add the brandy and ginger ale.

Irish Highball

½ measure Irish whiskey

Ginger ale

Dash of fresh lemon juice

Rind of a lemon

Pour the whiskey into a 10 oz tumbler filled with ice. Add the ginger ale and the fresh lemon juice. Garnish with a lemon rind.

Knickerbocker Special

¾ *measure white rum*

3 dashes raspberry juice

3 dashes fresh lemon juice

3 dashed of fresh orange juice

2 dashes of orange curaçao

1 pineapple chunk

Add the ingredients to a shaker half-filled with ice cubes. Shake and strain into a 12 oz slim jim glass. Garnish with a pineapple chunk.

Kon Tiki

½ *measure Irish whiskey*

½ *measure Bacardi rum*

Dash of Cointreau

Slice of lemon

Mix ingredients together in an iced mixing glass. Serve over ice in an old-fashioned tumbler. Garnish with a slice of lemon.

Manhattan

½ *measure rye whisky*

⅓ *sweet Vermouth*

Dash of Angostura bitters

1 cherry

Add ingredients to a mixing glass and stir. Serve in a chilled martini glass with a cherry.

Millionaire

¼ *measure dry gin*

¼ *measure sweet martini*

¼ *measure Kirsch*

¼ *measure cherry brandy*

Add the ingredients to a mixing glass and stir. Serve over ice in an old-fashioned tumbler.

Polo Club

¼ *measure Martini Bianco*
¼ *measure Kirsch*
¼ *measure Yellow chartreuse*
Dash of fresh lemon juice
Twist of orange rind

Add the ingredients to a mixing glass and stir. Serve over ice in an old-fashioned glass. Garnish with the orange twist.

Sidecar

½ *measure brandy*
¼ *measure Cointreau*
¼ *measure lemon juice*

Add all the ingredients to a shaker. Shake and strain into a chilled martini glass. Garnish with a lemon twist.

Baby Guinness

¾ *measure Kahlua*
¼ *measure Bailey's*

Pour the Kahlua into a shot glass. Holding a cold teaspoon upside down (and only just touching the surface of the Kahlua) slowly pour the Bailey's over the back of the spoon to create the second layer.

Slippery Nipple

¾ *measure sambuca*
¼ *measure Bailey's*

Pour the sambuca into a shot glass. Holding a cold teaspoon upside down (and only just touching the surface of the sambuca) slowly pour the Bailey's over the back of the spoon to create the second layer.

Perfect Lady

½ *measure dry gin*
¼ *measure peach brandy*
¼ *measure lemon juice*
Dash of egg white

Add the ingredients to a shaker. Shake and serve in a chilled martini glass.

Fallen Angel

½ *measure dry gin*
½ *measure fresh lemon juice*
2 *dashes of crème de menthe*
1 *dash of Angostura bitters*

Add the ingredients to a shaker. Shake and served in a chilled martini glass.

Urban Beauty

¼ *measure brandy*

¼ *measure dry vermouth*

1 *dash white crème de menthe*

1 *dash grenadine*

¼ *measure fresh orange juice*

1 *cherry*

1 *slice of orange*

Add the ingredients to a shaker. Shake and serve in a 12 oz slim jim glass. Decorate with the slice of orange and cherry.

Snake-in-the-Grass

¼ *measure gin*

¼ *measure Cointreau*

¼ *measure dry Vermouth*

¼ *measure lemon juice*

Add the ingredients to a shaker filled with ice. Shake and strain into a chilled martini glass.

Champagne Cocktails

Champagne Flute

1 lump of sugar
Dash of Angostura bitters
Chilled champagne
Slice of orange

Saturate sugar lump with the bitters and place in a champagne flute. Pour in chilled champagne. Garnish with a slice of orange.

French Fs

1 teaspoon of sugar
½ measure dry gin
juice of half a lemon
Chilled champagne

Add the gin, sugar and lemon juice to a champagne flute over crushed ice. Fill with chilled champagne.

Happy Youth

½ measure cherry brandy
juice of half an orange
1 lump of sugar
Champagne

Add the cherry brandy, sugar and orange juice to a champagne flute. Fill with champagne.

Bucks Fizz

¾ measure champagne
¼ measure freshly squeezed
*   orange juice*

Add the ingredients to a champagne flute.

Pimm's Champagne

½ measure Pimm's
Chilled champagne
Strawberry

Add the Pimm's to a champagne flute and fill with chilled champagne. Garnish with the strawberry.

Black Velvet

5 measures champagne
5 measures Guinness

Half fill a champagne flute with champagne. Top with Guinness. The Guinness must be settled before it is added and should be added to the champagne very slowly to prevent fizzing. If the head is too big, skim a knife over the top.

Index

A

Adams, Gerry **90**
Ahern, Bertie **90**, **106**
Aitken, Jim **14**
Allen, Woody **78**
Aquarius magazine **49**
Archer, Brian **115–116**
Asya, Zeynep **102**

B

Barbezet, M.M. **4**
Barden, Oliver **52**
Barman's Union of Ireland **105**
Beatles, the **21**
Beef Tribunal **106**
Behan, Brendan **26**
Benson, Des **52**
Bianconi, Charles **18**
Bird, Tim **33**
Bisset, Paul **48**
Blake, Rhona **55–56**, **74**
Bolton, Samuel **4**
Bonnyman, Jim **92**
Bono **2**, **53**, **89–90**, **102**
Bowen, Elizabeth **6**, **26–27**
Bowler, Gillian **111–112**
Boyd, Daragh **17**, **95**
Boyd, Etain **17**, **46**, **54**, **93**, **107**
Boyd, Josephine **17**, **66**, **104**
Boyd, Sean
    born, 10
    childhood, 11–12
    children, 17
    cocktail competition, 1967, 15,122
    family, 11–13
    sectarianism and, 12–13, 15, 16
    wife, 17

Boyd, Tom **13**
Brady, Charlie **40–41**, **81**, **83–84**
Breathnach, Maebh **42**
Brennan, John **11**, **86**, **105**
Braithwaite, Kate **85**
Braithwaite, Sir Roderick **85**
Browne, Gareth, the Hon. **21–25**, **56**, **84**, **88**, **93**
Browne, Tara, the Hon. **21**
Brown's **37**
Burke, Martin **2–3**
Burns, Mike **110**
Buswell's Hotel **106**
Byrne, Davy **115**

C

Caffrey, Oliver **53**, **67**, **89**, **108**
Cagney, James **2**
Campbell Sharp, Noelle **63–64**, **78**
Carmody, Simon **89**, **102**
Carroll, Des **113**
Carroll, Marie **113**
Carthy, Paul **54**, **87**
Cassidy, Frank **48**
Cassidy, Patrick **48**
Celtic Tiger **25–26**, **48**, **85**
Clinton, Bill **53**
Coates, Kevin **24**
cocktails
    equipment, 121
    history, 118–120
    recipes, 122–133
Cole, Paddy **52**
Cole, Virginia **46**, **64–65**
Collins, Michael **2**, **71**
Connaught, the **19**

Cooney, John **90–91**
Corr, Andrea **102**
Corr, Jim **102**
Corrs, the **102**
Cotton Jury, Margaret **5–6**
Cousins, Pat **38**
Coward, Noël **7**, **23**, **25–26**
Craddock, Harry **117**
Craig, James **35**, **47–48**, **67**, **96–101**
Cuddy, Mick **54**
Cummins, Simon **106**
Cusack-Smith, Molly, Lady **20**, **102**

D

Daily Mail, the **102**, **107**
Danaher, Gerry **106–107**
Davis, Derek **16–17**
de Burgh, Chris **101**
Delahunty, Mick **86**
Desmond, Dermot **74**
Devlin, Alan **57**
Dobbin's **37**, **39**, **112**
Doheny & Nesbitts **48**, **85**, **107**
Doherty, Pat **50**
Doyle, Aidan **116**
Doyle, P. V. **106**
Duane, David **65**, **66**
Duffy, George **32**, **65**, **77**, **82–83**, **121**
Dunphy, Eamon **45**, **59**, **72–75**, **82**, **103**, **114**
Dunraven, Lord **25**

E

Edwards, Hilton **23**
Egan, Dave **67**, **68**

Egan, Mairead **67–68**

Evening Herald, the **30**, **55**

Evening Press, the **60–61**

Express, the **107**

F

Fanning, Aengus **110**

Farrell, Michael **26**

Fennely, Martin **50**

Fields, W. C. **119**

Finnegan, Mary **23**, **63**

FitzGerald, Desmond (29th Knight of Glin) **23**

FitzGerald, Gareth **90**

FitzGerald, Olda (Madam FitzGerald) **23**

Flatley, Michael **67**

Fleishman, Hillard and Saunders **32**, **55**

Flood, Dr **65–66**

Flynn, Mick **55**

Forest, Christina **54**

Fox, Lucy (Lady Gormanston) **25**

Fox, Robbie **96–97**

Freud, Lucien **50**

Friday, Gavin **89**, **102**

G

Gallagher, Jim **18**

Gallagher, Patrick **48–49**, **65**

Geary, Tadgh **57**

Gebler Davies, Stan **62**, **107–108**

Gebler, Ernest **62**

Gibbons, James **102**

Gillespie, Paul **90**

Gormanston, Viscount **23**

Grace, Brendan **86**

Grant, Paddy **86**

Greene, Grahame **7**

Grenfell, David **25**

Guggi **89**, **102**

Guinness **86–88**

    200th anniversary **14**

    family **14**, **86–88**

Guinness, Brian **25**

Guinness, Desmond **24**

Guinness, Ernest **88**

Guinness, Mariga **24–25**

Guinness, Oonagh (Lady Oranmore and Browne) **21**, **88**

Gunn, Louise **54**

H

Hamilton, Mr **81–82**

Hand, Jim **52**

Hanly, David **89**

Harbour Lights Bar **11**, **71**, **86–87**

Hardiman, Adrian **106**

Harland and Wolff **16**, **50–51**

Harris, Richard **42–43**

Hart, Gary **49**

Hastings, Reggie **84–85**

Haughey, Charles **8**, **50**, **73**, **88**

Healy, Griffin **46**

Healy, Tom **54**

Heather, John **25**

Heeney, Bill **90**

Higgins, Alex **114**

Hill, Derek **26**

Holland, Mary **74**

Horseshoe Bar

    champagne and, 51–52

    opened, 7,

    business deals, 85 , 92, 97–98

    dealing with complaints, 42, 50

    design, 28–29

Horseshow Week **23**

Houlihan, Con **60**

Howard, John **50**

Howard, Patrick **50**

Hudson, Rock **8**

Humbert Summer School **49**, **90**

Hume, John **53**, **72**, **90**

Hurt, John **56**

Hynes, Dessie **49**, **62**, **95**, **103–104**

I

Independent, the **72**, **75**, **107**

Irish Press, the **59**, **60**

Irish Times, the **75**

Irvine, Jonathan **55**

Iveagh, Lord **88**

J

Jagger, Mick **23**

Jordan, Neil **71**

Jury, Captain Peter **6–8**

Jury, Colonel E.C. **6**

K

Keane, Terry **50**, **73**

Keaveney, Tom **54**

Kelly, Cyril **90**

Kelly, Kevin **52**

Kennedy, Jacqueline **8**

Kennedy, John F. **8**

Kennedy, Senator Edward **49**

Kilbracken, Lord **25**

Kilfeather, Sean **59–60**

Kindersley, Kim **88**, **93**

King, Llewellyn **90**

L

La Stampa **115**
Lavery, John **86**
Lawlor, Liam **63**
Lawlor, Vi **68–69**
le Broquy, Louis **26**
Le Coq Hardi **50, 74**
Lemass, Seán **2, 8**
Lenihan, Johnny **24**
Lenihan, Paddy (Junior) **14**
Lenihan, Paddy (Senior) **13**
Lennon, Jake **54**
Lennon, Pat **54**
Lillies Bordello **66–67**
Linden, Eddie **49–50**
Lord of the Dance **67**

M

MacLíammóir, Mícheál **23**
Madigan, Paddy **54**
Mahon, Geraldine **49**
Mahon, John **49**
Manning, Maurice **49, 103–104**
Mara, P. J. **71, 74–75,
88–89, 90, 93, 110**
Margo, Richard **51**
McAleese, Mary **13–14**
McAuley, Archdeacon **11–12**
McClory, Kevin **21, 60–61**
McColgan, John **46**
McColgan, Lucy **46**
McCormack, John **7**
McCoy, Arthur **35, 43,
69–71, 82, 113**
McCurdy, John **4–6**
McDonnell, Count Randall **21**
McDowell, Professor R. B. **24**
McEntee, Myles **55**

McGarry, Tony **90**
McGlinchey, Claire **80–81**
McGlinchey, Ian **66–67**
McGlinchey, John **65, 80–81**
McGowan, Gloria **23**
McGowan, Jack **23**
McGowan, Shane **62–63**
McGrattan's **112**
McGuinness, Dermot **106–107**
McGuinness, Martin **90**
McGuinness, Niall **63**
McGuinness, Paul **63,
74–75, 90–91**
McGurk, Tom **110**
McKeown, John **95–96**
McLaughlin, Brigid **107**
McLaverty, Bernard **12**
McNamee, John **93**
Mcnaughton, Gillian **102**
Melia, John **43–44**
Mère Zou, La **25, 37, 56**
Michael Collins, movie **70**
Minogue, Kylie **51**
Mitford, Diana **25**
Moore, Kevin **64, 68**
Moore O'Farrell, David **95–96**
Moran, John **49, 110**
Morgan, Dermot **71**
Morris-Lowe, Joshua **102**
Moyne, Lord **88**
Mulcahy, Mick **26, 75–77**
Mulligan, Paddy **58**
Mutless, Charles **55–56**
Murphy, Paddy **39**
Murray, Louis **115**

N

Neary's **57**
Neeson, Liam **71**
Nelson, Mr **73–74**
Newsweek International **8**
Nulty, Maureen **53**
Nulty, Oliver **53**

O

O'Brien, Denis **33**
O'Brien, Edna **62**
O'Byrne, John **37–38**
O'Callaghan, Barry **108**
O'Carroll, Mary **114**
O'Connor, Jerry **38**
O'Connor, Roderic **23**
O'Connor, Sinead **93**
O'Doherty, Michael J. **41**
O'Donnell, Mary Geraldine **24**
O'Donoghue's **30, 49, 94,
103–104, 112**
O'Hara, Blaise **56**
O'Kane, Frank **35, 38**
Olden, George **5–6**
old Hibernian, the **18**
O'Malley, Daragh **43–46, 61**
O'Malley, Dessie **106–107**
O'Neill, Elizabeth
19, 79, 89, 97, 110
Oranmore and Browne, Lord **21**
O'Reilly, Joe **110**
O'Reilly, Ronan **55**
O'Reilly, Tony **8**
O'Sullivan, Michael
23, 27, 56, 102
O'Sullivan, Sean **21**
O'Toole, Peter **2, 8, 43**

P

Patton, General George **10**

Pearson, Julian **102**

Pearson, Noel **37–39**, **57**, **93**

Philbin Bowman, Jonathan **82–84**

Pig n'Chick'n **16**

Previn, Soon-Yi **78**

Princess Grace of Monaco **8**

Prior, Aidan **29**

Pym, Grace **24**

Q

Queen Elizabeth II **7**, **55**

Queen Salote of Tonga **7–8**

Quigley, Fr Sean **54**, **85–86**, **108**

Quinn, Aidan **71**

R

Reed, Oliver **29**

Renard's **96**

Reno, Bob **91**

Reynolds, Albert **106**

Rickman, Alan **71**

Ricoux, Jean **51–52**, **80**

Roberts, Julia **70**, **93**

Robinson, Gerry **111**

Robinson, Mary **90**

Robinson Ryan, Donal **26**

Roe, Valerie **66**

Rogers, Michael **38**

Rolling Stones, the **21**

Royal Hibernian Hotel **15**, **18–19**, **84**

rugby **94–95**, **103**

Ryan, Ambassador Richard **36**

Ryan, Gerry **110**

Ryan, John **54**

Ryan, Paul **102**

Ryan, Tim **88**

S

Salmond, Alex **90**

Saunders, John **55**

Scott, Michael **7**

Shane, Noel **110**

Shelbourne hotel
  175th party, 6, 38–39, 109–110
  1999 history, 6
  architecture, 4–5
  blackout, 92–93
  Elizabeth Bowen history, 6
  history of, 1–9
  lockout, 103, 104–106
  modern hotel, 8–9
  'new' Shelbourne, 3–4
  opening, 2–3
  refurbishment, 7, 89, 103, 107–108, 109
  staff, 34, 90, 91, 96–97

Sheridan, Margaret Burke **7**

Siemer, Paul J. **33**

Smyth, Sam **17**, **75**, **88**, **91**

Souter, Camille **26**

Spilane, Timmy **71**

Spotlight **18**

Star and Garter **14–16**

Stephenson, Sam **29**

Stokes, Stephen **89**

Stuart, Francis **84–85**

Stuart, Ian **84–85**

Sunday Independent, the **73**, **107**, **110**

Sunday World, the **60**

Sun, the **55**

Sutherland, Kiefer **93**

T

tabs, **43–44**

Taylor, Ritchie **55**

Telegraph, the **107**

The Bartender **117**

The Berekeley Court **116**

The Burlington **116**

The Observer **75**

The Spectator **107**

The Sunday Times **74**

Tiernan, Rhona **74**

Trimble, David **90**

U

U2 **74**, **110**

Unicorn, the **85**, **112**

W

Wallace, Dr John **26**

Walsh, Pat **39**

Walston, Catherine **7**

Wanderly Wagon **46**

Welch, Sissy **78**

White's Tavern Wine Cellar **14**

Williams, Captain Jack **23**

Williams, Desmond **23**

Williams, Jane **23**

Wilson, Harold **8**

Woods, Ronnie **114**